NEAR DEATH TO

GRAM SEED
WITH ANDREA ROBINSON

CWR

Copyright © Gram Seed 2008
Published 2008 by CWR, Waverley Abbey House,
Waverley Lane, Farnham, Surrey GU9 8EP, England.
Registered Charity No. 294387. Registered Limited Company
No. 1990308. Reprinted 2009, 2011.

See back of book for list of National Distributors.

Unless otherwise indicated, all Scripture references are from the
Holy Bible: New International Version (NIV), copyright © 1973,
1978, 1984 by the International Bible Society.

Extract from Madness song 'Embarrassment' used by permission
of Hannah Management Ltd.

Concept development, editing, design and production by CWR.
Cover image: Boro TV Ltd.
Printed in Finland by Bookwell
ISBN: 978-1-85345-462-2

DEDICATIONS

I dedicate this book to Natasha, my wife, who sacrificed a huge part of her life leaving her mam Barbara, dad Brian and sister Naomi, her two brothers Heath and Lance and all her friends, who she is very close to, to obey what Jesus told her to do and that was to support me in Middlesbrough.

The work I do, I can do in a deeper way, because Natasha is behind me. I also want to mention our boys Caleb and Boaz, who have meant so much to me; Natasha is not just a loving wife but a great mum.

I love you Natasha.

Thank you for all you do.

To my mam who has had to put up with all the heartache of the way I behaved, and yet still when asked to switch off the machine that was keeping me alive, said 'No, keep fighting'.

Thank you, Mam, and sorry.

In loving memory of my nana and grandad.

Also in loving memory of Patrick Hinton, who was like a father in the Lord to me, whose wisdom and love got me through things like becoming a husband and a dad.

I believe Patrick saw this day, when a book would be released. I miss him.

This is Gram's story told from his point of view. We have endeavoured to include all the major events in his life, but we also recognise that we can't include every detail and incident – to do so would probably require a number of books! Because of Gram's former alcoholism and state of mind, he had gaping holes in his memory regarding his past and spent a lot of time prayerfully piecing it back together using discussions with friends, family and professionals who have known him. Therefore, while we have made every effort to ensure the accuracy of the information, we also recognise that there may be some omissions or accounts that differ from the information, perception and opinions of others. However, we hope that you will understand and appreciate the purpose of this book – to demonstrate God's power to transform a life and the ongoing mission of sowing seeds of hope in the lives of others.

God bless you.

Andrea Robinson

Andrea Robinson is a writer, former journalist, singer and songwriter, who currently works as a consultant (Career Management) for CXL and sings in a 70s disco band, Wonderboogie. She recently launched a personalised poetry and writing business, Have I Got Words for You! She lives in Blackpool and has three children – Daniel, Emma and Jessica.

CONTENTS

FOREWORD

Gram Seed is living proof that Jesus is alive and well and is still changing lives today. He has an extraordinary story to tell and I am so pleased it is now in print. Little over a decade ago, having spent many years in prison for various crimes, he was sleeping on a wooden bench in a Middlesbrough street, addicted to drink and drugs, cut off from his family and with no friends.

Then a group of young people from a local church befriended him and he was told about God's love. Later, when he fell desperately ill, they gathered around his hospital bed to pray for him. When they invited him on to an Alpha course he came to faith in Jesus Christ and his life began to change. Now Gram is a new man and has become a wonderful friend to many people around his Middlesbrough home and further afield. His kindness and cheerfulness often lead to him going out of his way to help people. He loves to tell others about God's love and has seen many lives transformed through his ministry.

Married with two young sons, Gram devotes his life to those in prison, going inside to tell them about what God has done for him. He has helped introduce Alpha* into a number of prisons and his ongoing ministry continues to bring hundreds of young offenders in touch with Jesus Christ. Gram is an inspiration to us all.

Nicky Gumbel
Vicar, Holy Trinity Brompton
*Information/contact details about Alpha can be found on p.176.

INTRODUCTION

Back in 1997, the Lord told me very clearly that I had to wait ten years before writing a book about what had happened to me. It was difficult at times – I wanted so much for everyone to know about the amazing things Jesus had done in my life – and I was approached by several people who wanted to write my story. But I knew I had to be patient; after all, God's timing is perfect. Yet again, He proved His faithfulness by allowing the opportunity to come up in the same year that I launched a new, independent charity – Sowing Seeds Ministries.

Waiting also allowed the Lord to build a solid foundation in my life, proving that these changes were genuine, permanent and not a flash in the pan – I'd seen others write their books and before they've even gone to print, they are back to their old ways.

Working on the book with Andrea has been both painful and healing. I'd told my story many times, but some things I'd not talked about in such depth before, and some I'd never told anyone. They had been buried for years and were too painful to face. But as we discussed the horrible things I'd done and the people I'd hurt, God began to bring a lot of buried rubbish to the surface. Often on the long journey back from Blackpool after meeting Andrea, I cried so much that I had to stop at the side of the road. But they weren't tears of regret – they were tears of release as the Lord finally healed me of so much from the past; the presence and love of God was overwhelming.

By reading my story, I hope and pray that you will learn, like me, just how much Jesus loves and forgives you, no matter what you've done, and through that you will find real hope and a life worth living.

THANK YOU ...

Andrea Robinson. This book will touch people all over the world because of your dedication and hard work. I want to thank you very much for the way you have written my life story. Thanks to Andrea's husband Mark and family for supporting her while writing this book. Simon Page for getting the ball rolling and introducing Andrea to the project – thank you Bro.

Martin and Margaret Ruddick. For inviting me to your house in 1996, and making me feel that I belong. I want to thank you both for the ten years of discipleship you gave me, the thoughts and wisdom you spoke into my life. Thank you.

Phil and Sally Hillsdon. Thank you for supporting us as a family and for your kind words of wisdom. Jane Hinton. God bless you Jane from all of us. You are such an example of Jesus, thank you for being a spiritual mother to me. Albert and Pauline Dicken (Goshen Trust). Thank you for your love and support for my family and myself. You have been with us from the very start of the prison ministry, and when you prayed for me in 1999, when the prison ministry seemed a long way off, and beyond me, you had faith in what I was doing and what the Lord was saying to me. God bless you.

Peter Conroy, and Aiden Poulter, who faithfully prayed for me at the hospital and came to visit me, they showed me the love of Christ in a practical way. Thanks to Peter and Helen Conroy for welcoming me into their family.

All the people who I have not yet met, who prayed for me and are still praying, we are so very grateful.

I would like to acknowledge and dedicate all of my life and future to Jesus Christ the Son of the living God.

God bless you
Gram

FADE OUT

It wasn't supposed to end like this. He had his whole life ahead of him. But now even the medical staff have lost hope.

He once had the world at his feet – rich, popular, powerful, strong. Now that striking twenty-one stone of muscular physique has shrivelled to a filthy skeletal frame – barely moving, barely breathing. Not even eight blood transfusions could stop the rot from years of self-abuse.

The once-white hospital sheets are thick with dirt from his unwashed skin. The room is deathly quiet, apart from the relentless bleep of the machinery that is keeping him alive – for now at least.

How did it happen? It's an all too familiar story. Let's freeze the moment – delay the final scene for a little longer – and rewind.

Stop there: that's him, slumped on his bench – home for the last three years – clutching another bottle. Those filthy, stinking trousers and thin, vomit-stained T-shirt are already stiff with frost. He'll soon be scavenging from bins to relieve the agony of hunger. He was once a match for anyone – now he's too weak to fight off the daily torrents of abuse and beatings. He hates what he's become, but his only escape – twenty-eight pints of White Lightning a day – no longer numbs the pain. It's all he lives for now.

He passes the time reminiscing about what he used to

be. You wouldn't recognise him. Go back again – stop. Yes, that's him, surrounded by his crew – tanned, toned and on top of the world. His gangster connections are reaping rich rewards. Dressed in Armani and dripping gold, he has his pick of women, using them and discarding them at will – no regrets, no remorse. He's conning the town and raking in the cash. It's a dangerous game – one he's about to lose.

Take it back one more time. This is the soundtrack of his childhood – screaming, crying, shouting, the sound of someone choking – and, finally, silence. There he is, huddled on the stairs, tears running down his face. The ambulance has left. It's all over, but nobody explains to him what's just happened. He's just a boy. He knows his family is different – he's lived with the taunts and rejection for as long as he can remember. But it's all about to change. The pressure is building up to boiling point. The battle is about to begin.

Let's fast forward once more to his final moments. He's deteriorating quickly now. Friends and family have said their goodbyes – their words falling on ears that no longer hear. That's his mum by the bed, keeping watch over the son she loves – the son who has broken her heart so many times. The doctors are with her now; they want to turn off his life support. He's no longer responding. There is nothing more they can do.

So there we have it – another tramp, another hospital – and another wasted life. The scene is about to finish and fade. Let's leave it here – we don't need to see any more. We don't even need to know his name.

But these guys knew it – in fact they've been looking for him. Everyone else had given up on him – a dirty, stinking drunk who launched vicious verbal attacks on anyone daring to approach his bench – but they didn't give up. They spent endless hours listening patiently to his drunken ramblings, understanding his suffering, his desperation, offering him the only glimmer of hope in what was left of his life. He was suspicious; it had to be a set-up. Nobody gives 'owt for nowt'.

They missed him. Now they've found him again – and want to change the ending. They know they are helpless, but that powerful, invisible force that motivated a desire to reach out to a dying alcoholic is ready to kick in again. Here they go, approaching the bed, laying hands on him, and praying. But what's the point? He's as good as dead already ...

#

CHAPTER ONE

WHO AM I?

'Graaaaam, where are you?'

We were looking for newts in a nearby field when I heard my nana calling me.

My mate, Haisey, looked up from the pond.

'Seedy, what's that your nana's shouting? It sounds like Gram.'

I was christened Graham, which was my nana's maiden name, but she struggled to say it properly without her teeth in.

'Gram sounds good. Why don't you use it?' suggested my mate. 'Don't you think it's better than Seedy?' He was right. Seedy sounded like a kid's nickname. Gram carried more weight. It sounded more grown up and at seven years of age I desperately wanted to be like my older mates. But then I desperately wanted to be anyone but me.

My mam wasn't happy. 'You can't call yourself Gram. It's disrespecting your nana.'

She's always used my birth name, even to this day.

Gram, Graham, Seedy, Alio (my 'holiday name'), they were all me, but who was I really? Since my birth – 28 April 1964 in Carter Bequest Hospital, Middlesbrough – part of my identity had always been missing. Throughout my childhood and early adulthood, I felt that I didn't belong anywhere. I believed that I wasn't loved or accepted. I was a psycho, a scumbag, a waste of space, a troublemaker. But no one really understood what was going on inside – the real me behind the masks.

I'd lived with my nana and granddad, Billy and Pat Gaunt, since I was a baby. My mam, Pat, married a heavy drinker, who used to hit her and steal her money. The last straw came when he married another woman and was convicted of bigamy. He was sent to jail and my mam saw it as a good opportunity to get rid of him. She moved back in with her parents and brothers – Terry, John and Derek – when I was nine months old.

I never knew my dad, but I was always very curious about him. I often wondered if different people were my dad and no one was telling me. Was it my granddad, and my mam was really my sister, or was it our Derek, because he was big and blond like me? Who was really who?

Sometimes I blamed myself for what had happened. Suppose my dad hit my mam because I came along? They were very young; maybe he couldn't handle a kid crying or having another mouth to feed. Maybe he just didn't want me around.

I felt I had to keep all this to myself. My dad had become this big family secret that we didn't talk about. I tried to find out, but nobody would tell me; my questions were brushed aside, subject changed, secrets kept hidden. Growing up I saw other lads spending time with their dads – even the ones who didn't live together would meet up at weekends – but where was mine? Finally, after overhearing the truth one day about what my dad had done to my mam, that seed of curiosity started turning into anger; an anger that became so great that it drove me, at sixteen years old, to storm into his local pub, high on drink and magic mushrooms, with a sword down my trousers. I was going to kill him.

My nana and granddad lived in a rough part of Middlesbrough called Ellerby Green, at Berwick Hills. Home was a small semi-detached house with three bedrooms and I had to share a bed in the box room with my mam. I moved into my uncles' room when I was old enough.

I was quite close to my uncles, especially our Terry, the youngest, who I called Kidder. They even said I could call them my brothers, but I knew it wasn't the truth. Their appearance, behaviour and relationships with their parents were different from mine and I felt left out and very jealous. Even when my mam remarried, my surname wasn't changed and I'd never been given the same one as my uncles and grandparents. I was the only Seed in the family, named after a man I would never know and who never wanted to know me. It was part of my 'proof' that I was a reject and didn't fit in.

Because of my jealousy, feelings of isolation and confusion, I became very rebellious. I instigated a lot of fights in that house. I used to turn my mam against my grandparents and my uncles against each other. Sometimes it was all too much for my mam. One night, after a big argument with my nana and granddad, she grabbed me, put me in a car and took me to a flat. This happened a few times and she would return home when things had calmed down. I didn't really understand what was happening, where we'd gone and why – I was too young. But I felt the tension; a feeling that stayed with me through most of my childhood.

My granddad was the authoritative figure in the house and everyone respected him as that. He was very strict and sometimes bad tempered, especially with me when I got into trouble. He seemed to be this massive guy with big shoulders, although when I got older, he actually looked quite small. I heard stories that he was a good fighter and I think he'd sorted my dad out a few times. My uncle Derek did a lot of weightlifting, so I used to think if he could sort our Derek out, he could deal with anyone.

He worked for British Steel as a ladle man. He stood at the top of a large barrel, testing molten steel and had to wear thick, protective clothing in unbearable heat. He was paid well, but had to work long hours as the main breadwinner. He would then spend most evenings and weekends in the pub.

Even though I didn't see him much, I enjoyed the times when it was just the two of us. We'd go for long walks and he'd tell me about his war experiences; he was a medical officer's assistant and part of the crew on the D-Day landing boats. As a teenager, he took me boxing and watched me play rugby – that meant a lot to me. He bought me my first dog, Sabre, to help me cope with a difficult house move and we took him out together. We had some great times. One day that stands out in my mind was when I was about ten. We went hunting for newts. We spent so long exploring the countryside that we got lost. We asked Sabre to take us home – and he did! I will always remember coming over the hill near our house and spotting my mam hanging out the washing. It was so reassuring to see her there. I didn't know it at the time, but she would soon be gone for good.

Granddad did everything for me a dad would do. I often wished he was. I even tried to call him Dad a couple of times, but it didn't work. It just didn't hang right and I felt embarrassed; what was I trying to do? He wasn't really my dad and never would be.

And then there was my nana.

*   *   *   *   *

'Get me out of here! I want to get out!' Nana jumped up off the sofa and rushed to the locked front door.

'Here we go again,' muttered my granddad. 'Calm down,

Pat. Come and sit down. I'll make you a cup of tea.'

By now she was desperately searching for the keys. She thought she was still in hospital – the place where they'd cut open her head, drugged her up and given her electric shocks.

My nana had her first breakdown during the war while my granddad was away. She was left on her own for two years with a baby. Later, she was diagnosed with depression, but I think there was more to it than that. She constantly heard voices that told her she was no good and had to kill herself. She would get bad headaches, fits of depression and these attacks where she would suddenly try to escape.

I often heard her having conversations with someone, but when I went into the room, she was by herself. She'd also shoplift for things she didn't need. She said the voices told her to do it. My granddad and mam would return the items to the shop; I suspect the shop owners were aware of the situation and that's why the police were never involved.

She didn't work and spent weekdays in St Luke's Hospital, Middlesbrough, where they gave her all sorts of medication and treatments. She had EST (Electric Shock Therapy) a number of times and once they cut a hole in her head to try and relieve some of the pressure on her brain.[1] I went to see her after the operation; half her hair had been shaved off and she looked so frail and vulnerable lying in that hospital bed. I loved her so much and hated what they were doing to her. It was barbaric, just one experiment after another, but nothing ever seemed to work.

To look at her, you wouldn't think she was ill; she appeared quite normal, although she would lose weight very quickly and then balloon out again. She smoked forty cigarettes a day and coughed constantly. She also drank a lot at the weekend. She and a friend from St Luke's, who I knew as Auntie Phyllis, would have two bottles of Navy Rum and twenty-four cans of Norseman lager between them. Auntie Phyllis would often wee herself and sit there smelling of it. My nana took Largactil (used to control psychotic illness) and would fall asleep. Once in this state she started choking on her false teeth and I had to put my hand in her mouth to get them out.

My granddad and my mam did most of the shopping and cooking, but my nana would try to cook at weekends. We had to keep a close eye on her because she would often leave things turned on and forget, or make mistakes. Once while making mushy peas, she took the salt tablet upstairs when she went to the toilet. She put it down and picked up a Sterident tablet instead that she and my granddad used to soak their false teeth in every night. Suddenly Granddad shouted, 'Pat, what have you done?' She'd put the Sterident tablet in the mushy peas, so we nearly had anaemic mushy peas and salty teeth!

And then there were the fights. I remember once sitting in our holiday caravan watching in stunned silence as the contents of the kitchen cupboard smashed against the wall – my nana and granddad were arguing again. We went to Flamingoland, in North Yorkshire, every year, but it was often difficult for my nana; we'd try to go out, but she often wanted to go back to the caravan. She'd just sit there and my granddad would have to stay with her. I never really understood what all the fights were about, but I know there was a genuine love between them and she relied on my granddad so much. However, I think he sometimes got tired of it all. He worked long hours, had four children to support, my nana's illness and my bad behaviour to cope with. No wonder he spent so much time in the pub.

I had my own way of escaping the conflict on our summer holidays; I became someone else – Alio. I would take on the character of this imaginary boy who was happy and had a normal family. I felt I could fit in and nobody saw me as a troublemaker. But then I would have to go home and become Gram again.

My nana was a royalist and had pictures of the Queen all over the house. She was also unbelievably religious. She always wore a cross, attended church at Christmas and Easter and was often in her bedroom looking at the crucifix and praying. Her room was quite eerie and the curtains were always drawn. That was my first experience of Jesus; just another imaginary character in my nana's head.

As a family, we carried the stigma of nana's illness; a lot of the neighbours thought she was mad and we were treated a bit like the Addams family. I often wondered whether my family were embarrassed by her. I wasn't, but there was so much I didn't understand. My mam and uncles must have been affected by it all their lives, but nobody ever talked to me about it and I didn't feel I was allowed to ask. More secrets. I would sit listening on the stairs and catch snippets of information – that's how I found out about my dad. I would then go to the bathroom and play with water, something I used to do a lot, while tears ran down my face. I felt so insecure and on edge.

But there was always one time of the year when everything was different: Christmas. I loved it; everyone was together, decorating the house, buying presents, eating and drinking. There were no arguments and, for that short time, it almost felt like we were a normal family. But when Christmas finished, everything was back to how it always was. I hated that; to this day I still get emotional when Christmas is over. Even when I found out there was no Santa, I willed it to be true because it was something to believe in.

With everything that was happening, what I wanted was

explanations and reassurance. What I got was sweets, crisps and other treats. My insecurity convinced me that they were doing this to keep me quiet and stop me asking questions. Even so, I still got a feeling of release from eating. Often, I couldn't stop and it meant I got quite chubby and was teased about it. I was often on my own and didn't make friends easily. I didn't know how to be close to anyone and I never stuck with friends for long.

It was because of loneliness and the need for comfort food that I first began to steal. I used to go to the corner shop with my pocket money to buy sweets and crisps, and grab some more on the way out. In my mind, I wasn't doing anything wrong. It meant I had more money for the next day and would gather a few friends round me as well, because I had so much.

Once I went into the nearby Newcastle House pub and nicked what I thought was a bag of crisps when the barmaid was in the back. It turned out to be a cash bag with about £50 inside. I tried to spend it at the corner shop, but the owner saw the bag and informed the landlord. I was caught red-handed.

We used to play around the estate and get up to all kinds of mischief. We kicked our ball against garages and got complaints about it. We collected spiders and used them to scare people, especially girls. We'd sneak into neighbours' houses and hide them in beds; I would try and stay awake at night to hear the screams as people threw back the bedclothes, but I never managed it. Our house was by an alley, hidden behind a fence, with garages at the end. I got up to all sorts down there, but when I went home, my granddad would shout: 'What were you doing there? I saw you hit that kid.' I had no idea I could be seen from the house.

I started at Ormesby Infants School later than other

children, but right from the start I was very disruptive. My desk was made to face the wall away from everyone else and eventually I wasn't allowed in the classroom. I sat in the cloakroom on my own and didn't do much work. I was too lazy to learn to read and write – something which affected me well into adulthood.

But as I got older and started junior school I got worse – much worse. I'd had enough. It was time to start fighting back.

---

1. St Luke's is a small psychiatric hospital, opened in 1898 as Cleveland Asylum. It was changed to St Luke's in 1926. **Electroconvulsive therapy (ECT)**, also known as **electroshock**, is a treatment that induces seizures with electricity. It became widespread as a form of treatment in the 1940s and 1950s, most commonly used as a treatment for severe depression and occasionally for mania, catatonia and schizophrenia. A more refined version is still in use today. **Trepanation** is the practice of boring a hole in the skull for medical reasons. One of the oldest medical practices, it has been used in modern times to try and relieve symptoms of mental illness. It is now largely disregarded as a pseudo-science, with no scientific evidence to support its claims.

CHAPTER TWO

FIGHTING BACK

'You're a fat — '

'You're nana's not right in the head. You're all a bunch of loonies.'

'You still believe in Father Christmas? You big baby!'

'What do you mean he's your dad? It's your granddad, you liar!'

They were laughing at me again. I could feel my anger building up and had no idea how to get rid of it, so I lashed out. This happened a lot and often my mam was called to the school. She used to get really upset with me. I don't think she knew about the teasing; I didn't tell her or my nana because I was trying to protect them. I didn't want them to feel hurt.

I spent a lot of weekends on my own in a room above a pub. My mam was downstairs doing relief work and if I needed anything I just had to pick up the phone. It was great, but what I really wanted was time with my mam, not pies, peas and bags of crisps. I missed her.

I loved being with her and always felt insecure when she wasn't around. I once stopped with her friends over the road – Auntie Sylvia and Uncle Les. I couldn't sleep because I was so unsettled. I went downstairs to find some food and then sat on my bed until morning. Sylvia always had chocolate biscuits; we couldn't afford to buy them and had to make our own. I was often over there eating them. I wasn't very nice to their children though. Their son, Craig, was into making model aeroplanes and I was into smashing them! He'd spend hours building them and I would crush them in seconds.

One night, when I was about seven, I was woken by the sound of an ambulance. I rushed downstairs and it was chaos; everyone was running about, shouting and crying. It was my nana – she'd taken an overdose. Granddad was holding her and trying to put salt water down her throat to make her sick. I was frightened and I didn't understand what was happening. I was told to go upstairs.

Suddenly she was gone. It was really strange in the house without her and, once the ambulance had taken her away, I didn't see her for another month. I felt so powerless and didn't know what to do or say. I constantly asked my granddad if she was coming back and what was wrong with her. I was told she was ill and nothing else.

Not long after she came home, it happened again. I sat on the stairs listening to the commotion and the anger.

'She's not done it, she's not taken anything.'

'She's just doing it for attention.'

Sometimes I would lie awake in bed and hear noises: shouts, bangs, cries. Unanswered questions, no explanations, more secrets – day after day. I was unsettled and on edge, but I had a new way of coping. I'd learned, somehow, to push it all to the back of my mind and replace it with something good, something to look forward to. I was starting to put on masks to hide my real feelings. And it would be a long time before they came off again.

The day we left our old home will always stand out in my mind. I didn't want to go, but I didn't have a choice. We moved a few miles away from Berwick Hills to Springbank

Road, Ormesby. I think my granddad wanted to improve life for my nana by moving to a better district. It was a much nicer area, surrounded by woods and hills, but the move made me feel even more isolated. In Berwick Hills most people had social problems and many children didn't have their dads around. In Ormesby, everyone seemed to have parents, brothers and sisters, good jobs, nice cars and businesses. I began to realise just how different we were as a family. I didn't fit in. I felt like a freak. I buried it and put on another mask.

I didn't get on with my neighbours. There were three girls next door and I was really nasty to them. I chased them and put frogs down their backs and, if they played with their tent in the garden, I would climb in and knock it down.

The lad on the other side of us, Stuart Cuthbert, used to call me names. I was still fat and a slow runner and he was very fast. I couldn't catch him and used to hate him for that, but I also envied him. He was really good at football and had lots of friends.

One day, I caught him and bust his nose open. I suddenly felt this great relief, like I had some power over him and the situation. After that whenever I hit him, he'd go and get the local bully, Steve Sizer, who was about four years older than me. Eventually I managed to punch him as well, which stunned him a bit. We'd often end up fighting, but eventually became friends.

One day, a bully from another estate attacked me.

I wasn't going to take it any more; I hit him and he hit the floor! The next day, everyone started talking to me and asking me to play football with them. I realised it was because I'd hit this bully and from then on I started fighting a lot more. My uncle Terry was absolutely mad about Bruce Lee, and I watched the films with him over and over again, practising the moves. It became part of me, that need to fight, to have some power, to be the best; that's how I thought you got friends and became popular.

I could handle the local bullies now, but I couldn't protect myself from everyone. One night I was in bed asleep and a family friend came into the room and dragged me down off the top bunk by my hair. I woke up in fright and he kicked me between the legs and bust my face open. One of my uncles caught him hitting me and he was thrown out of the house. I was really upset and angry and I had no idea why he'd hurt me; I wondered what I'd done wrong. I never found out. It was never discussed.

Another time I was messing about in the snow with my mates; we used to knock at people's houses and when they opened the door we would throw snowballs at them. Once we did it to this bloke who was known as a bit of a nutcase. He came running after us and caught me and my mate. He dragged us down his drive, smacked me on the head and made us take the snow off his wall with our little fingers. I couldn't fight him off because he was so strong. I told him my granddad would sort him out, but when I told my granddad, he didn't do anything. Years later I smashed this man's windows and hit him, but that first event had a big effect on me. I started fighting back more and didn't bother telling my nana and granddad. No one was coming to help me; I had to look after myself now.

*   *   *   *   *

My mates were laughing at me. I was coughing, spluttering and trying to catch my breath. I felt sick. I was ten years old, enjoying my first cigarette! Once I'd started smoking, I carried on, even though I thought it would kill me; my nana said that 'if you smoke and swear at the same time you'll die'.

I was doing both.

I started nicking cigarettes from my nana and granddad; my granddad used to hide them from everyone, but I'd always find them.

At that age, you don't realise that something tried in all innocence as a bit of a laugh can eventually destroy you – like my first drink. It was New Year's Eve. We were quite close to the River Tees and at midnight the ships blasted out their horns twelve times. There was a great party atmosphere and everyone was on the streets and in and out of each other's houses. I found a can of lager, tasted it, and didn't really like it. However, the next day, I took one from under my nana's bed and drank the lot. I'd never felt like that before – all giggly and happy inside. I enjoyed it so much that every weekend after that I nicked one of my nana's cans, or some of her rum. I also started helping myself to the drinks cabinet. One time, me and Steve Sizer drank his dad's whisky. I'd eaten loads of chocolate and crisps and after four mouthfuls of whisky I threw up on the floor. We got into big trouble; Steve said it was all my fault and his dad, who was a bit of a madman, came looking for me.

Then one day my dog Sabre disappeared. He was a lovely black Alsatian and he had become my best friend. He'd gone missing before, but this time he didn't come back. I was so upset and I used to cry about losing him; I was teased for that as well.

Someone told me that the local farmer had shot and killed him. I had to get my revenge, so I set fire to his barn with a cigarette. What I didn't know was that there was chemical fertiliser inside. I ran back to my street and suddenly heard a massive explosion and the corrugated iron roof blew off. The fire crew arrived. I was never caught for that and I felt as if I'd got the farmer back.

All this time, my mam was working hard and trying to

better herself. While she was working at a local club as head barmaid, she met a man who was to become her second husband. Dave Lawson was a schoolteacher with a nice car and treated my mam really well. However, I felt very insecure and was very hostile towards him. I wasn't going to let him take my mam.

On their wedding day, I was kitted out in new clothes, but inside I just felt really strange. Everyone, including my mam, looked so happy and we were all together, having a great party. I got drunk to blank it out. I was losing my mam. I couldn't cope.

She showed me a council house, about a mile away from my nana and granddad's house, that I thought was going to be my new home. I was torn; I didn't want to leave my nana and granddad, but also wanted to be with my mam.

I even helped her decorate, still not knowing what was going to happen. However, it soon became apparent that she was moving there with her new husband – without me. I was to stay with my nana and granddad. I saw it as a massive rejection and missed my mam terribly. Even when she was working long hours, she would still come home at nights, but now she wasn't going to come home any more.

I hated my stepdad. I almost hated him more than my dad because he'd taken my mam away. I was determined to get back at him. I would lie and say he'd hit me. If he ever shouted at me, I would shout back that he wasn't my dad or my granddad and couldn't treat me like that. I was very angry, bitter and depressed.

I only slept at their house once. When I was in bed, I heard them talking and laughing in the next bedroom. They sounded like they were having fun and I felt so angry. I cried myself to sleep that night.

By the time I was eleven, my physique had started

changing. I was no longer a podgy kid; I was growing taller and stronger. I was ready for secondary school. I wanted to go to Ormesby County Modern (now Ormesby Comprehensive School); my friends were all going there, it was ten minutes from my mam's and I thought I could spend lunchtime with her. However, she sent me to Nunthorpe County Modern (now Nunthorpe Secondary School), which had higher grades and a better reputation. I think she wanted the best for me, but I saw it as another rejection. I thought she didn't want to see me or have me near her house. You start thinking these lies and they get bigger in your mind. It became another reason for my rebellion.

Every night when I finished school, the most important thing was to get to my mam's as quickly as possible. The time with her was so precious and I wouldn't let anything get in the way. Teachers tried to keep me back at times, but there was no way I'd let them. It was about two miles away and took about half an hour to walk. I ran if I missed the bus and got uncontrollably angry about it; I even stole motorbikes and children's pushbikes to get there quicker.

I also had to go past this estate where children from a rival school lived. Often I fought gangs of them on my own if my mates weren't around.

I used to arrive at my mam's about 4.30pm on weekdays and we had tea and watched *Happy Days* together – my step-dad disappeared into the bedroom out of my way as soon as I arrived. Mam left for work and I walked home, crying all the way.

I'd do anything to see her. I went on Saturday morning and she often sent me to the shops or to get fish and chips for lunch. Often there were older lads hanging around who would beat me up. They threw bricks at me. One put a fag out on my hand once; another beat me in the eye and bust my lips and nose. (When I was older and stronger, they wanted me on their side.) I'd go back messed up and my mam would have a go at me for fighting.

Sometimes she left a key for me to let myself in on a Sunday (especially if my nana was cooking!). My mam had nice food in because they had quite a bit of money. They even had Sugar Puffs. I'd never seen them before. I would go in, lock the door, shut the curtains and have a fried egg, a Dale steak and chocolate biscuits. It became a routine way of life.

But my life was far from routine. It wasn't long before I found myself, at twelve years old, trying to restrain my nana while granddad poured salt water into her mouth. She'd taken another overdose. There was no doubt that she'd done it this time; she'd taken everything she could lay her hands on.

It was chaos again, but this time I was part of it. She was screaming and trying to knock the salt water away. It went everywhere; her hair was soaking wet, her eyes were red from the salt and her face was really white. She tried to clamp her mouth shut and at one point, she was almost limp.

'Pat, open your mouth,' my granddad shouted.

I hated having to restrain her. My uncles, who had left home by then, suddenly arrived with my mam and took over. I escaped into the next room and shut the door. I tried to block it out of my mind again, but this time, it wouldn't go. I could still hear all the screaming and yelling. Someone shouted:

'She *has* taken 'em, there's the bottle!'

I could hear her being sick.

'She's choking!'

The ambulance arrived. I thought she was dead.

She had more electric shock treatment. I went to see her in hospital, but she didn't recognise me. Granddad said, 'Pat, it's our Gram,' and she stared at me, confused, as if I was a stranger and said, 'Who? Who's this?'

I turned and left. As I walked down the corridor, I felt so hurt and angry about everything. My mam had got married and had a new home without me, all my uncles had gone, there was just me and my granddad left in the house and now my nana didn't know who I was.

Right then, leaving that hospital, I made a decision: I wasn't going to let anyone hurt me anymore, either emotionally or physically. I'd had enough and I was sick of it. To everyone else, I was still the same Gram, but inside it was building up behind the masks; I was like a bottle of lemonade, shook up, with the lid on, waiting to explode. Slowly, but surely, I was getting ready to erupt.

CHAPTER THREE

YOU'RE AN EMBARRASSMENT

As soon as I heard it, I knew. I knew they were talking about me.

> *You're not to come see us no more*
> *keep away from our door*
> *don't come round here no more*
> *what on earth did you do that for? ...*
> *You're an Embarrassment*

I was a big fan of Madness, but as soon as I heard 'Embarrassment' in 1980 I immediately thought of it as my song. It summed up what everyone – family, teachers, police and neighbours – thought of me.

'You're a scumbag. You'll never amount to anything.'

'You'll never get a job. You'll spend the rest of your life in prison.'

'I don't know where I've gone wrong with our Graham. I've always done my best for him. Why has he turned out like this?'

'What have you been up to now? You'll kill your nana with your behaviour.'

'Please don't be like this, son, because it really hurts me.'

It went straight over my head. I'd switched off. Nothing or

33

no one could affect me now. I was determined to prove them wrong though, but all I ever did was prove them right.

It was all a bit of a laugh, to start with. By the age of twelve, I was nicking off from school and having bets with my mates over who could steal the most stuff. Once I managed to get 101 bars of chocolate in one day from different shops. Sometimes it was pints of milk, milk money off doorsteps or clothes from washing lines.

I shaved my hair off and started knocking about with a skinhead gang. Up until this point, I'd had shoulder-length blond hair – almost white. My mam's friends would often say: 'Ooh, look at his hair. Isn't it lovely!' I wanted rid of it.

I'd stay out really late getting into trouble. Nobody knew. My mam wasn't there any more, my granddad was out working or at the pub and my nana was knocked out with her medication or drink. What did they care?

By fourteen, I'd discovered drugs – magic mushrooms that grew in the nearby woods, cannabis, glue, petrol sniffing – anything that would get me a bit high. Many of my mates became seriously addicted, even dying from overdoses, but I think what prevented me going the same way was my nana. I'd watched her take drugs all my life and seen the effect on her. Deep down I just wanted to be like my mates. What really took hold of my life was alcohol; it made me fearless and got rid of the pain and thoughts of rejection.

Some nights would find me and my mates at the local youth club, playing pool, listening to music and eating sweets. All very normal … apart from the fact that it was 3am and we'd broken in through the skylight! Sometimes we'd attended some of these clubs, doing what the youth leader wanted, listening to his music, not ours. Now we were in control; we could do what we wanted, play what we wanted, nick and eat what we wanted and laugh about it the next day.

By now I was nicking anything I could. I took motorbikes and pushbikes to travel around on. I'd steal a lot from my stepdad – money, sweets and cigarettes. It was my way of getting one over on him.

I had no fear of the police – that was part of our code, even though my granddad had tried to teach me to fear and respect them. I'd first got in trouble with them when I was twelve for nicking a pushbike. I'd also been done for being drunk and disorderly and trying to nick a car, using a spare set of keys we'd salvaged from scrap yards.

I tried to keep it all from the family. But my granddad knew. He kept a lot hidden, because he didn't want to upset my nana. That became quite a weapon for me. So did my nana's illness. I was nicking off from school all the time, but I would get nana to write sick notes for me. She didn't have a clue what was happening. I would always ask her while she was waiting to go to hospital.

'Nana, can you write me a letter? Remember when I was off school ill last week?'

'Oh, right. Yes … OK, son.'

I was lying, of course, but how was she to know?

I even manipulated the school secretary into giving me letters; I said my nana was ill and she needed to see something to prove that I was attending.

I was, officially, the worst pupil that Nunthorpe County Modern had ever had – that's what the police were told. I was often kept out of the classroom, but I would just wander off somewhere. I didn't do much work and I used to get my brother's girlfriend to do my homework for me; I'm sure they knew it wasn't mine. I got the cane or the slipper nearly every day (which was common in those days) but I laughed at it. The headmaster, who was also a local magistrate, whacked me across the ear once. I pushed him over the desk and he hit his head on the radiator. I never felt anything, because I'd turned my mind against the pain. My mam sometimes hit me with rolling pins and metal pans to try and knock some sense into me, but I laughed at her as well. She used to get really upset with my behaviour and wonder where she'd gone wrong with me.

But there was one thing I really enjoyed at school, one thing that I would even attend lessons for: sport. I loved it. One of the teachers, Mike Wright, was the captain of Middlesbrough Rugby Club. He asked some of us to come and train at the club. My eyes lit up; someone had actually taken an interest in me! I started playing for the junior team, often on a Sunday. My granddad came to watch and my mam came once with her friends – on the one occasion I knocked the referee out. I came out of a scrum and ran straight into him; they had to bring in a replacement. She said: 'That's typical of you. I come with all my friends and you knock out the referee!'

I also played rugby at school and was asked to play in goal for the school football team. However, it meant that I had to go to lessons those days and I was told if I only turned up for sport and not classes, I couldn't play.

I loved boxing as well. The training helped to build my physique. By this time the puppy fat had gone and I had started to get a lot more muscle, so I wasn't the slow runner I used to be. Improving my shape, and having people show interest in me, really made me feel good about myself. My granddad took me boxing and that meant a lot. It felt good when it was just me and him.

But after a few years I started enjoying life on the street more, being part of the skinhead gang and fighting. I also couldn't get drunk the night before a game – I could only have a shandy – so I dropped out of all sport. Even as a young teenager, drink was starting to control my life.

There's a real sense of security and belonging in a gang, especially when you have something in common. A lot of the lads I knocked about with were in the same boat as me, having unsettled childhoods. They had no foundations or security, so they looked for it in other ways – what they wore, the car they drove, the gang they hung out with, the house, the girl, the crime. I had always felt like an outsider in my family and community; now, with mates I identified with, I finally felt like I belonged somewhere.

A lot of my mates were older than me, which meant I had more expectations to live up to. They were used to drinking, taking drugs and committing crime, so even though I had only just started out on that path, I automatically jumped up to their level. But I never became as bad as my mate Wogo.

*   *   *   *   *

'There's a copper behind us! When he pulls us up, drag him into the van and we'll cut his head off.' Wogo was serious. He had a six-inch knife to prove it.

We were driving across the moors in a clapped-out old transit van with blacked out windows – fifteen skinheads going to Scarborough.

Amazingly, the police didn't stop us.

I'd been mates with Wogo (Anthony Watson) since I was thirteen and I really looked up to him. But from an early age, I knew he was on a self-destruct mission. Nothing was good unless it was bad. He climbed up scaffolding when he was drunk. One night, he broke into a house because he needed a tin opener; another time he nicked a colour portable TV and swapped it for a packet of fags. Once he found a drunk unconscious on the floor and robbed him of his gold, emptied his pockets and even took his shoes.

One night we were in his stepdad's car and suddenly I could hear boots thudding behind us on the road – stable boots with lace ups and metal tips, popular with fighters. In them was his stepdad.

'I'm going to kill you!'

'Wogo, put your foot down! There's a big meathead after us!' I shouted. 'What's up with him?'

'I've nicked his car.'

'Wogo, man, you're doing my head in!' I thought he'd just borrowed it. We parked round the corner and legged it. I didn't go round to the house for about a month after that.

Deep down he was a good lad. We used to talk for hours and I realised that, like me, he'd had some bad breaks and was lashing out at everyone. But he became far worse than me. Years later, I was in the Jack and Jill pub when a mate called me and told me to turn on the TV. Wogo was on the news; he'd climbed fifteen floors up, between two closely-built blocks of flats, and was at the top, refusing to come down. I knew he was violent towards girls, but now he was accused of murder. He was caught, found guilty and sentenced to life.

I visited him in prison and he seemed like the same old Wogo, not bothered about anything or anyone. He told me he'd taken acid the night before and gone to a pub in Middlesbrough. He used to have these out-of-body experiences on drugs. He was losing it. I knew he'd eventually self-destruct. I was right; this was the last time I would see him alive.

*   *   *   *   *

By the time I was sixteen, I was robbing from everywhere – community centres, shops, garages, sheds and schools. I got a 50cc motorbike especially for the job. I planned it all carefully, slipped out the house when my nana was asleep and hid the gear until I could go back for it the next day. I often walked by expensive cars and took golf clubs out of the boot. They were rarely locked and I thought that if they were daft enough to leave a car open, they deserved to lose their stuff.

I didn't think I'd get caught, but I came close to it at times. Once, when nicking stuff from our school's technology department, I heard a dog bark. I hid behind one of the big desks and the school caretaker, Mr Bollins, appeared nearby. His dog was sniffing near the window and I really thought I'd get caught – that was a big adrenalin rush – but they disappeared. I was a bit reckless sometimes though. Once I broke into my school and sprayed my name all over. The police thought I was innocent, because nobody would be that daft!

That adrenalin rush, as well as money from selling the gear, was what I loved. It was daring, exciting and my way of hitting back at my past. I had a huge chip on my shoulder about what had happened to me; it had all been outside my control. Now I was in control. It was quite a change from how I was as a child, nervous and mixed up, even though I appeared to be confident and rebellious. However, all this never made me truly happy. I was never satisfied with whatever I had. I always wanted something else, something more.

I was thought of as a bit of a psycho. I would wander through woods alone at night and in parts of Middlesbrough that even my toughest mates wouldn't go near. I had a fascination for ghosts; one local hospital was considered to be haunted so, of course, I had to break in to an old abandoned wing and wander round alone, in the dark. I had no fear.

In my eyes, I wasn't a bad lad. I was loyal to my mates, said please and thank you, was respectful to older women, in honour of my nana – granddad always taught me never to hit a woman. I also never robbed houses, which was considered to be the lowest of the low, even in the criminal world.

So really, I was OK – wasn't I?

I would never let anyone get close to me, especially girls. I could get loads of lasses, but I treated them like dirt, especially my girlfriend, Angela.

I met her when I was fifteen. She was my first real girlfriend. My nana wasn't too impressed. I introduced them in a pub one night and she said to me later, 'She's a lovely lass, but I don't like her hair!' Angela was a punk, with black, red and green hair and a ring through her nose. I had no hair at all. We made a lovely couple!

I was with Angela for about six years and, even though I loved her, I treated her like a dog. I slept with other girls and told her that she wasn't as good as them, or they were slimmer and had nicer clothes. She'd arrive in nightclubs to meet me and I'd be 'slapping the lips' of (kissing) other lasses; she'd storm out – I think she felt embarrassed and used. Sometimes she threw drinks over us. But I had no remorse.

I think she put up with it because she really loved me and thought she could change me. Sometimes I wanted to change for her, but it didn't last. Once I got arrested for non-payment of fines. It was Saturday night and I was feeling very sorry for myself; all dressed up and nowhere to go but a police cell. Angela came down and, because she'd dropped everything to come and see me, as she'd always done, I decided there and then that I would change my life for her. I sat in that cell all night thinking about it: I was going to spend the rest of my life with her; I'd never get into trouble again; we'd get married; I'd get a job.

'Mam, it's Gram. I'm stuck in Middlesbrough police station. Can I have £120 to get out?'

My mam put the phone down on me. I tried again.

'Mam, I'll go to jail on Monday if I don't pay it. I've got a job interview Tuesday. I don't want to miss it.'

There was no interview, of course, but she believed me. She sent the money over with our Derek, who gave it to Angela to pay the fine. I took her out that night and told her that I loved her and was going to change. However, the next morning, everything I'd said meant nothing. My words were cheap and I went back to my old ways.

But, of course, it wasn't my fault that I behaved like this. I blamed everyone and everything else – especially my dad. He'd abandoned me; he'd knocked my mam about; he deserved to suffer for it. And I was going to make sure that he did.

CHAPTER FOUR

I FOUGHT THE LAW – AND THE LAW WON

I burst through the door of my dad's local, high on drink and magic mushrooms, with a sword hidden in the back of my trousers.

'Is Derek Charles Seed in here?' I yelled. The place fell silent.

I'd still never met my dad, but my mam had told my mate, Maca, to keep me away from the Brambles Farm Hotel, because it was my dad's local pub. Maca told me. For weeks I brooded about it and the anger built up. I knew I had to confront him.

As I stood in the pub that night waiting for him to appear, one of the bouncers approached me, took me outside and said: 'Don't do it, son. You'll go to jail for the rest of your life.'

I was glad the next day that I hadn't seen him. Once I'd sobered up and calmed down, I began to realise that what I knew about him was only second-hand knowledge, but I was angry at everything and everybody; I needed an excuse to take it out on someone.

I found out later he'd seen me around Middlesbrough and was scared of me, especially after that incident. I also found out I'd lived near his daughter – my half-sister – for about eight years; I'd passed by her house so many times and never known. Her family were scared of me, too.

But everything was about to change ... or so I thought. It wasn't long after leaving school that I found myself sitting in front of the interview panel at British Steel, wearing my brand-new suit that my mam had bought me; I'd even grown my hair to look more respectable. I was going to be offered an apprenticeship. My granddad and our Terry worked there, our Derek was on the selection panel; the job was mine – my chance to settle down and sort my life out.

I was told they'd let me know when to start so I waited to hear from them. And waited. And waited. They never called me back. I never found out why. It was more rejection, more reason for carrying on with my way of life. They didn't want me. What choice did I have?

By this time I'd been in the police station thirty-three times and in the juvenile court seven times for being drunk and disorderly, for breach of the peace, and for theft and criminal damage.

However, the police now had evidence on me robbing from schools and youth clubs. I'd been seen coming out of one place and they had found fingerprints and other evidence elsewhere. They had also checked my history and tied me in with a lot of other break-ins. They had a very strong case against me.

The worst I'd had so far was five cautions and a fine of £4.50 for criminal damage, which was paid at about 50p a week. It wasn't much of a punishment. However, now I'd been charged with twenty-two counts of burglary and my solicitor said that because it was so serious, there was no option other than a custodial sentence.

That weekend, I went into town for a goodbye celebration. I was back in court the following Friday and, even though there was a chance I could get off with a suspended sentence, it looked like me and this other lad in our gang were both going down. We started early. We were out all day drinking and fighting lads from another town at Redcar Racecourse. By night time, we'd forgotten about these other lads and we ended up in a punk and skinhead nightclub called the Rock Garden.

Above the Rock Garden was another club called the Marimba (now called the Arena). The police had insisted that the Rock Garden closed at 1am and the Marimba at 2am, so the two crowds didn't clash. However, by the time we left the Rock Garden, we spotted the lads we'd been fighting that day coming out of the Marimba. A big fight broke out and instead of the seven of us from earlier, there was now about fifty. More and more people joined in. It must have been a scary sight – a mass of mohicans, bald heads, big boots, safety pins and pink and green hair!

The coach these lads had come on from the racecourse was nearby. We chased them onto it and it suddenly started moving. I thought I'd better jump off in case the police came, and I ran back to the entrance. Suddenly everyone started screaming and it was almost as if everything was in slow motion. Even now, if I shut my eyes, I can still hear the screams; it's something you never forget.

Everyone was just stood there, staring in my direction. As I looked down, there was a body with no head on the ground in front of me and it was shaking. I turned and ran.

I caught up with my friend and said: 'I really feel something bad is going to happen to me. I can sense it.'

We went to his house and I sobered up very quickly. I usually slept at his place every weekend, but this night, I just sat there.

At half-past six in the morning, the phone rang. It was Granddad.

'The CID's been here. You need to come home,' he said.

'They won't tell me what it's about, but it's very serious. What have you done? You're going to kill your nana with your behaviour.'

I said: 'Please, Granddad, don't tell her. I promise I'll tell you the truth when I come home.'

I knew my granddad wouldn't believe me; I'd lied so many times. The week before I'd been in the police station again, emptying my pockets, when out fell a pair of green knickers. Embarrassed, I said to my granddad that a band at the nightclub had thrown them into the crowd. He believed me.

It wasn't true. They were from a girl's house in Whitby. One of my mates was in bed with her, and me and my other mate were drinking and nicking presents from under the tree. He took these green knickers and tied them to the aerial of his car. On the way home, he was arrested for drink driving. One of the gang threw the knickers in the car, but I thought we'd better not leave them there, so I put them in my pocket – until they ended up in front of the desk sergeant.

My friend came the next morning and told my granddad the truth about the knickers, that I'd not actually nicked them. He was trying to help, but my granddad found out I'd lied again.

It was a long walk home that night. All I kept thinking was: poor Gram, I'm going to go to jail for a very long time. I never once thought about the lad who died or if he had any family. I was just consumed by me.

As soon as I arrived home, the street suddenly filled with police cars and I was hauled off to the station. I was under suspicion of murder. I tried to tell my granddad what had happened, but he didn't want to know and wouldn't come with me.

I was taken down to the cells. There were fifteen of them and every one had Doc Marten boots outside. I thought I would somehow be all right then because there were loads of our lads there.

I was put in a cell with some skinheads and punks. One had smuggled some cigarettes in, so we sat smoking and talking. They asked what had happened and I said I didn't know. I even lied to them. I'd been off my head when it happened and started to believe that I must have been guilty of something. I felt I had to lie to protect myself.

For five days, I faced endless interviews. The police said they had statements from witnesses who said I'd thrown this lad under the bus.

'We're going to get you for murder, so you might as well tell us the truth,' they told me.

'I am telling the truth. I didn't do anything.'

'You're a liar,' they shouted back, over and over again.

It didn't help that my friend came down to say I was with him when it happened. I wasn't, I was on the bus. They kept him in for eight hours.

I was dazed by it all. Previously, being locked up was a laugh, but it wasn't funny any more. Then I started having regrets:

'Why couldn't I have another chance?'

'I wish I hadn't gone out that night. I'll never do anything bad again.'

There were a lot of us who were accused of having a part in this lad's death, but all the police had were statements from drunks. Finally the truth came out. The driver had seen all these punks and skinheads running towards his coach and, scared for his life and the other passengers, tried to drive away. He hit this lad, who got turned over on the road and hit a signpost. The bus ran over his head and shot his body further away. The driver was charged with drink driving.

I felt I'd escaped a life sentence, even though I was

innocent. I then began to believe I was unstoppable. I thought then that even if I did get into trouble, as long as I didn't kill anyone, I would never get as long in prison as I thought I was going to get. That night had a big effect on me, but I carried on as if nothing had happened. I just put on another mask.

Back at court the following Friday I had butterflies in my stomach, wondering what was going to happen. I was angry with myself for feeling like that, but I tried to act tough and cocky, pretending I didn't really care. I wondered whether the lad's death would be brought up, but they couldn't mention it because it wasn't anything to do with the burglaries.

The magistrate glared at me as I stood in the dock. 'Graham Seed, you think you can behave how you like, but you can't. You can't continually step over these boundaries. You have to learn to abide by the rules. I'm going to sentence you to nine months in Medomsley Detention Centre.[1] You will have plenty of time to think about what you have done.'

I'd heard about Medomsley from other lads who had been there and I knew exactly what I was about to face. I was gutted.

1. Medomsley Detention Centre, in Consett, County Durham, was built in 1898 and acquired by the Prison Commission in 1959. It was known for its 'short, sharp shock' treatment of young boys and a 1977 inspection report described it as 'Dickensian'. It was closed and demolished in 1983.

CHAPTER FIVE

ON THE FRONTLINE

I was lying at the bottom of the metal stairs, trying to stop the bleeding from the hole in my head. My tooth had been knocked out, my eye had started to close up and I had suspected broken ribs. I couldn't move properly for weeks afterwards.

At the top stood the two prison officers who'd pushed me down. It was my fault, of course; I'd sworn at them and answered back. I deserved it, especially after everything I'd done in the past. I deserved to be punished.

My medical treatment? They threw me a towel to mop up the blood. Nothing more. The official line was that I'd tripped. And they made sure I was kept away from visitors until the injuries had healed.

It was what I'd come to expect from Medomsley Detention Centre: boot camp discipline, insults, brutality, excessive punishments, icy dorms, rock hard beds. Years ago, it had been a Victorian workhouse and I think it kept the same spirit – and the same level of suffering. It changed me. I was a different person when I came out. I was much worse.

Being locked up for the first time was a big shock to my system. My daily life had been getting up when I wanted, going where I wanted, taking what I wanted and going to bed when I wanted. Suddenly all that was gone. I kicked off a few times, but I quickly learned to do as I was told, mainly because I wanted to eat. I found out that if you didn't behave, you would just get a piece of bread and jam and some water.

We had to be up at 6.30am every morning. Everyone was in eight-bed dorms which were so cold in winter that they had ice on the insides of the windows; the old heating pipes produced hardly any warmth. The beds were hard and the mattresses were so thin that all you could feel were the metal frames underneath. We had to fold back the bedclothes into little squares each morning. We then had to run round the outside fence in all weathers, wearing a vest, shorts and pumps. If you were wise, you didn't run in your underpants because if it was raining, they'd get soaked; you'd then be in them all day.

We were so frozen when we came in that even the cold showers felt warm. We would then put on our uniforms, have breakfast, parade in front of the governor, and go to our work duties. Mine were mixing cement and carrying bricks. By 7.30pm, we were locked in the dorms and the lights were turned out at 8.30pm. We had an extra hour at weekends.

The prison officers were sadistic; they were determined to make our life hell and seemed to enjoy hurting us. It was supposed to be tough, but they'd been given an inch and they took a mile. We were treated like dirt, with constant shouting, insults and humiliation. Sometimes work duties were turned into punishments. Corridors had to be swept with a small hand brush; if a spot of dirt was found, or if an officer walked past and left boot marks, we had to do the whole corridor again. If we complained, they made us clean the toilets or sweep outside. I remember one lad being forced to cut the grass with a pair of scissors and others were made to dig deep holes and fill them in again with the same mud. One lad had to do that every day for a week.

But the worst thing was the violence. If we answered back, they would smack us across the face, punch us in the stomach or whack us on the head. One officer had a rubber tube to whack us across the legs or the backside on the early morning run; sometimes he hit us so hard that we had red stripes across our skin. But they were also very crafty. Sometimes they would put a mattress over us and hit us, so it didn't leave any marks. If one of us got badly hurt, they would keep that person hidden until those injuries had healed. No medical treatment or painkillers were offered.

At first, the staff tried extra hard to intimidate me in front of others, because I was a newcomer. However, I knew some of the lads there and, because I was also athletic, people wanted me on their side in team games, so I soon fitted in. Once I got my feet under the table, I started getting the best sleeping arrangements and perks like extra mattresses from the lads in stores.

The only fights between lads were over possessions like soap, stamps and toothpaste. We were given 75p a week to buy essentials. Fights were never about territories or what someone was inside for; although a couple of nonces (sex offenders) were battered in the showers with mops once, after the officers tipped off some lads about what they'd done.

We were allowed one visit a month. Only Angela, my girlfriend, came; my granddad was very disappointed in me and my mam didn't want anything to do with me when I was in prison, so they never came. They kept it from my nana because of her health. She thought I'd gone to London to find work.

That Christmas was dismal. They made a bit of an effort, a few decorations and a Christmas dinner, but that was all. I was so depressed; I missed my nana terribly. I thought of all the wonderful Christmases before, with the party atmosphere and all the family together. I stopped caring about Christmas at this point; it became a chance to get drunk and dressed up, rather than a time to be with loved ones.

The one benefit of being in Medomsley was that I got very healthy. The air was really clean in Consett and we were running outside every day. I also stopped smoking; you couldn't get that many cigarettes anyway.

To this day, Medomsley was the worst prison I've ever been in. It may have worked for a lot of lads, but it didn't work for me. When I got out in February 1981, after four months and four days, I was a different person. I was more angry – angry at the system and angry at myself for being such a failure. I made another decision: I definitely wasn't going to do anything that anyone told me ever again. I was free to do what I wanted.

I woke up the next day still in Medomsley ... in my head. Despite my hangover, I still half expected to be shouted out of bed. In fact, mentally I was still locked up for about a month. I used to talk about it all the time: what I would have been doing at different points in the prison day. I was buzzing; I'd done it, I'd done time, just like loads of my mates had.

I promised my nana I would get myself sorted out with a job. Amazingly, I was true to my word and a few weeks later I was on the pork floor at the local slaughterhouse hauling lumps of meat around. It was a good laugh; some of my mates worked there and a girl I liked worked nearby. I felt like I was earning an honest living. That was something new! It was a YTS (Youth Training Scheme) and all I got was £23.50, working from 6am until 4pm, five days a week. I used to make that in an hour selling gear. After three weeks a rumour started that they were getting rid of everyone the following week. I'd had enough; I thought, why wait another week? I might as well leave now.

My next job was as a petrol pump attendant, but I felt like a fool because I knew some of the people arriving in cars. I was embarrassed. I lasted a day and a half.

I told my nana both times that the manager had accused me of stealing, rather than admit I gave up. She believed me, but every time I tried something and failed, it made me sink lower. But it wasn't long before I had a new passion: football.

I'd watched Middlesbrough FC a few times as a lad with my uncles, but this time it was different. The crowds, the noise, the excitement – the atmosphere was amazing. There were so many memorable matches:

Middlesbrough v Bolton Wanderers – stabbed in the arm and chest four times
Middlesbrough v West Ham – face slashed with a double-edged Stanley knife
Middlesbrough v Everton – sliced with a knife, just missing my throat and cutting off a chunk of my chin
Middlesbrough v Leeds United – face and eye ripped open by a police Alsatian dog

I was also hit over the head with a blunt, sword-like instrument that left a long, deep gash in my skull, had four front teeth knocked out and had a bottle stuck in my eye and chin. And I loved it!

How did I get into this? I had become bored of being a skinhead by then; all we ever did was drink in the same clubs and fight in the same pubs. One night, not long after my seventeenth birthday I was roaming around and met some lads from the Frontline (sometimes known as the Frontline Service Crew), who were the 'firm' following Middlesbrough.

'Why don't you come to one of the matches with us?' one of them asked me.

'Nah, I'm not too bothered about football. It's for wimps,' I told him.

'Yeah, but there's loads of fighting.'

I didn't need asking twice.

Every football team had its own 'firm' – gangs of football hooligans who follow specific clubs. Flickheads followed Liverpool, so-called because of their wedge haircuts; the Casuals were linked to Halifax; the Inter City Firm (ICF) followed West Ham; Chelsea had the Chelsea Headhunters and the Chelsea Smilers – well known for inflicting the Chelsea Smile, which involves slicing rivals' faces on either side, like a permanent smile (a trick copied from the Kray twins).

The aim of the game was to give the other side a good kicking. It became an all-day mission; we started early in the morning waiting for the other side's firm, followed them round and fought them in the streets, in pubs, outside the grounds, anywhere we happened to clash. It became a mass scuffle, charging into each other, trying to stand our ground, inflicting as much damage as possible on the enemy.

I dismissed the violence because to me, it was war; both sides knew there was a risk, but they set out to attack and to win. I never walked past an innocent bystander or family member and hit them. We only went to hurt people who wanted to hurt us. The police tried their best to intervene. Often visiting fans were given a police escort, us included, but firms would slip away to go and fight.

It got nasty at times. In the seventies, when it first started, it was all about throwing a few punches, but by the time it came to the eighties, knives and other weapons were involved. During one match against Nottingham Forest, a Middlesbrough supporter got killed. I was nearby when it happened. But it was something new, something exciting. I had a new interest, a new set of friends and a new way of dressing. I'd turned my back on my old skinhead mates. They didn't want much to do with me any more.

In between matches, we rifled nearby shops, especially if we were away from home; we thought we had a bit of anonymity. When matches weren't on we went to all-night clubs playing northern soul.

On Sundays, hundreds of groups met at Stewart Park, Middlesbrough and sat around all day smoking dope, playing music and chatting up girls.

You got to know your own gang and what they wore: southern gangs wore better clothes and ski jackets; Chelsea gangs often wore suits. We wore designer tennis or golf clothes – never football. We watched Wimbledon and attended fashion shows to check out what was being worn and visited shops in London. Our message to the world was: 'Look at us, look how smart we are. We're not scum' – even though we acted like it.

My first attempt at copying the trend was a disaster; I was clueless. I bought some horrible cheap trainers and a really daft jumper from Asda, with a diamond pattern on. And there was everyone else in top designer gear! They said it was better than my skinhead gear, but I knew I'd have to make more of an effort. I decided to go 'shopping' at a local golf course. I entered the shop, still wearing my Asda jumper with the sleeves down to hide my tattoos, and nicked some designer jumpers. I then stole some jeans from town for me and my mate. I had to buy the trainers; they were kept in boxes at the back.

It was easy to steal from the golf shop; they weren't expecting a thief. It then became a new way of getting quick cash – travelling round golf clubs, stealing gear and selling it on. I'd finished with break-ins; that was all kid's stuff. I'd gone into the bigger league; I was a better class of criminal now.

*   *   *   *   *

Middlesbrough had a new shop. It was full of designer gear and became so popular that people were queuing up outside the door. They thought they were buying the genuine articles. The seller was my mate and the shop was his back bedroom. I became his assistant. We were bringing new fashions into Middlesbrough, but it wasn't long before it became a big underworld operation. Local gangsters were opening warehouses to make counterfeit gear. They would buy thousands of Lacoste badges and labels from Thailand and sew them onto cheap £1.50 polo shirts, selling them for £10. I joined in on a smaller scale. I would secretly cut the labels off designer jumpers in shops (the jumpers were wired up to security alarms), sew them onto cheaper shirts and sell them. Medomsley had done me some good after all – it taught me to sew!

By now, making money was a full-time job. I travelled the country, stealing and selling. I went into arcades with 'foilies', which were 10p pieces wrapped three times round with foil; the machine treated them like 50ps and gave change. I also did 'stonking' which was sticking a crochet hook into a coin slot. The machine issued credits, which I played until the machine was empty. In addition I was given money by my mam and my nana, and I was also claiming dole.

Aside from my 'job', my motto in life was to achieve four things each day: have sex, get intoxicated, fight and steal. That's all I lived for. It was my life and I was doing exactly what I wanted. I still didn't think I was that bad. But I was about to commit what I considered to be my worst-ever crime.

One day, as I left the house, my granddad was struggling

home with some shopping bags. He saw me and shouted: 'Aren't you going to give me a hand?' I went on the defensive over the way he spoke to me, said no, swore at him under my breath and walked off. I caught his eye and saw such a look of hurt there. I didn't care.

I knew he wasn't well. He'd been reading books about cancer; I think he knew how serious his illness was, but he didn't say very much. He collapsed out of the bath a few times, but he told me it was high blood pressure.

A few months after that, he was in hospital having a routine operation for a blockage in his bowel. I was on the grass verge outside the house with two of my uncles, fixing a motorbike, when the phone rang. Our Terry answered it and said he had to go and meet our Derek. I knew that something was wrong.

I went off to have a fag and drink nearby with some mates and the next minute several cars arrived at our house. My nana and my mam got out and they were holding each other. I ran down the bank so fast I nearly fell over. I started shouting at them to tell me what was going on.

'Granddad's dead,' Derek said.

I ran off to the woods nearby and just sat there, staring at nothing. All I could see was his face and the pain in his eyes when I'd refused to help him that day. If only I'd have known how ill he was; if only he had told me.

Nothing I'd done up to this point – the violence at matches, robbing, lying, rebelling, treating women like dirt – compared to this. This was someone I'd loved and respected all my life and had had some brilliant times with, someone who had acted like a dad towards me. Yet at the point when he was dying, I'd let him down, just as I'd done time and time again. I hadn't even visited him in hospital; I was too consumed by my own stupid selfishness.

Our Terry came to find me and took me back to the house. I wanted to cry but I couldn't. I refused to cry at the funeral; people would think I was weak. I couldn't be weak. I was a tough lad. But inside, I was dying.

Granddad was being cremated and, as the coffin went through the curtains, I realised that I would never see him again. I just kept torturing myself with that shopping incident, playing it over and over again in my head. I'd hurt him so much; what if he'd thought he'd done something wrong that caused me to be so bad, when really it was only my own stupidity that caused it all?

I would often lay on my nana's bed, thinking about him. I kept trying to make myself cry by thinking of something upsetting, but I couldn't. My emotions wouldn't come out; I didn't even know whether there were any left.

For a couple of weeks after, the family were really close, grieving for my granddad, even though some of them blamed me for putting so much pressure on him. After that, they all disappeared and it was just me and my nana. I had to try my hardest to be good for her now. My granddad was gone and it was up to me to look after her.

At first she was really ill. We feared she wasn't going to make it. My granddad had always been there for her and we didn't know if she'd cope without him. She withdrew inside herself, drank more and took more medication. She kept my granddad's ashes in her bedroom like a shrine and she spoke to the box every day, especially on a Sunday. Once a girl I brought home said she smelt aftershave and I think it was my granddad's; my nana must have been putting it on.

Soon after, my mam became the manageress of a hotel in Durham. She'd been working hard for many years to get a job like this and I think she'd actually turned it down a few years before, so she could be around for me. The hotel provided a big cottage in the grounds for her and she took my nana with her. There were plans for me to join them at first; everyone thought a different area might keep me out of trouble. But yet again, my behaviour put a stop to that. I used to visit my nana every week, but I robbed the hotel and was still stealing from my stepdad. I had to be closely monitored.

I lived on my own in my nana and granddad's old house until it was sold. I was homeless for a while and slept on our Terry's sofa. But no one was around to keep an eye on me now, so I got worse. I carried on fighting at matches, and during a home game against Bolton Wanderers, I was arrested and locked in the cells all weekend. I was convicted of affray (rioting). While waiting for pre-sentence reports, I turned eighteen. I was expecting a long sentence because Medomsley hadn't changed me. However, somehow my records got lost between the juvenile and magistrates court. There were no computer records then and my solicitor didn't mention my previous convictions. My past had been erased and instead of about two years, I got six months in borstal.[1]

I was back inside, having to face one of my greatest fears – dying alone, behind locked doors. What if I had a heart attack? What if nobody came to help? I couldn't just walk out to the nearest doctor. I also worried about what was happening on the outside. What if something happened to someone I cared about and I wasn't there for them? You get really paranoid and fearful in prison. I once got a letter from Angela, who told me she'd met my mate, Kenny, in Blazers nightclub. He wanted to say hello to me and said he was looking forward to seeing me again. She also said she loved me and was missing me. I re-read that letter again and again and before long, I'd convinced myself she was having an affair with Kenny. I felt trapped and powerless.

I was in Deerbolt, at Barnard Castle, North Yorkshire. Deerbolt was run a bit like Medomsley – we wore uniforms and had a routine – but we were treated with a bit more respect. There were some big lads in there, eighteen- to twenty-one-year-olds, and the staff wouldn't have got away with the same brutality. Some of the officers were really nasty though; they'd antagonise us deliberately to make us feel bad.

I knew a lot of the lads from home and Medomsley. In fact, sometimes in the exercise yard, it was just like being in Middlesbrough town centre, apart from the fact we couldn't get out!

The lads still fought about possessions, cigarettes or cannabis. I've always said to people before they go to jail: 'Don't lend anything and don't borrow anything; you end up having to pay more back. If you borrow an ounce of tobacco, you've got to pay back an ounce and a half. If you don't pay it that week, it goes up to three-quarters the next.' Some ended up owing loads, even if they'd only borrowed a bit.

The fights could get pretty nasty sometimes, but I kept to myself and they left me alone, which was probably a good job; I was 6ft2 and weighed more than fourteen stone. I worked as a gym orderly, so I spent all day cleaning and helping with the equipment. It got me out of the dorm and kept me busy so the time passed pretty quickly. I was still a bit rebellious though. I would pass things on between lads in the gym and charge them and throw clumps of mud and grass around outside; once I threw a lump with a stone in it and it hit an officer on the back of his head. Everyone laughed.

I was nineteen when I left Deerbolt. I couldn't wait to get back to football matches. I knew one day I'd get caught again, but I thought it was somehow meant to be. Jail wasn't a deterrent, especially as a lot of my mates were there; plus, the life I was living was more attractive than the fear of going to jail.

I had a new name now: the Fila Boy (after the designer label). Sometimes I would be pointed out in the crowd; it made me feel really important. I was even on TV once – 1983, when we played Arsenal. I had to be there in my smart tracksuit; only a couple of people in England had that one. I had status and importance. That's what you needed to be liked and accepted. Or so I thought.

I still tried to sort myself out occasionally. The hotel where my mam worked was owned by Marion and Mike Adamson, who organised catering at Sedgefield Racecourse. As a favour to my mam, they offered me a job labouring, and transporting catering food. I worked in the morning and then hung around all day in case anyone needed more stuff. It was really good money and we got tips from the punters, but once again I messed it up by getting drunk. I always managed to abuse anything good. It was almost like it was too good to be true and I was waiting for something bad to happen.

But by Christmas, I'd found my ideal job: sitting in a pub, drinking, selling and making loads of money. My mate Lee's dad, Tommy Harrison, was involved in selling counterfeit gear. He asked me to get involved. I'd done this before with my mate, selling gear from his back bedroom, but Tommy's set-up was on a much bigger scale. This time, my own back bedroom ended up full of designer copies of Lacoste, Fila, Ellesse, Sergio Tacchini, and copies of Opium and Chanel No. 5. There wasn't a lot of designer stuff in Middlesbrough back then, so most punters didn't have a clue that they were copies. Those that did weren't too bothered because they were getting stuff cheaper.

Sometimes people would buy up to thirty T-shirts and one hundred Chanel No. 5 bottles at once, especially at

Christmas. I also had lads selling for me, so both Tommy and I would get commission. Some weeks, I'd be picking up as much as £3,000 on a Saturday.

I also travelled all over England as a driver for some of the local gangsters who controlled a lot of crime in the north-east, particularly the fraud, which was now on a huge scale. You always knew who the gangsters were (not because of their trilbies and machine guns!). They looked quite normal, but had a very powerful presence about them.

Now I had money. I bought extravagant presents for my mam, my nana and Angela. I'd bought my own house on Herbert Street, North Ormesby with the cash and money from my mam, through my granddad's will. I had a top-of -the-range stereo system, a smart leather settee, a nice car, gold rings on every finger, Rolex watches and a wardrobe full of designer clothes. We were going to London to buy the genuine articles with the money made from selling the fakes. I got taxis between pubs and sometimes took crowds of friends to restaurants and paid for all the food and champagne.

I was successful. I'd made it. I was nineteen years old, with piles of money, possessions, power, status and respect. But inside I felt so sad. It wasn't making me happy and I couldn't understand why. Looking back, I think I'd hurt so many people and messed up so much, but I didn't want to face up to it. I tried again to push it to the back of my mind behind a new mask – material success. I'd escaped into a new life and identity, but deep down inside I just wanted to be me. The problem was, I still had no idea who I really was.

I would often feel lonely and unsettled. One night I told Angela not to meet me. I was going to see another girl. I decided not to go in the end and I went home about 1.30am. I changed, had a drink, but after about half an hour, I wanted to go out again. I ended up in a taxi office chatting to a radio operator for four hours before I was tired enough to sleep. I had everything I could possibly want materialistically, yet I had to go and talk to a stranger to relieve the loneliness. It wasn't the first time, or the last.

Restless and unhappy, I decided to go to London. I'd done this before; I'd first gone when I was fifteen with my mate Maca to escape the police. We'd tried to find a skinhead shop called The Last Resort and then another shop which sold speciality Doc Marten boots with fourteen lace holes in them. Then as we walked along we'd noticed that there were no white lads any more; loads of black lads started coming out of the shops and staring at us. Cars started following us. We'd kept walking as fast as we could and managed to get away, but could have easily been killed. I never got my boots.

This time, I was going down to get a job – another stupid idea of mine. Some lads I knew had told me about all the work down there and the money that could be earned. I travelled down, met some of the lads and had a chat with a construction site foreman, who offered me work on his site for £80 a day, cash in hand. At 11.30pm that night I was on the bus home. I had suddenly wondered what on earth I was doing there and decided I couldn't handle it.

When I got home, my mam was cleaning the house for me. She was shocked to see me back so soon and I lied and said there was no work for me. I also told her I had no money and she gave me some. My mam didn't mind helping me out, but I think she preferred me out of the way. I'd hurt her so much I don't think she could take any more. She knew I was up to something dodgy, but maybe she tried to blot it out. She'd tried so hard all her life to do the best for me, even though I'd convinced myself she didn't care.

All this time, the police had been watching. They knew I was up to something. I think I'd been under surveillance for a few months, but I thought I was too crafty for them. I'd load the car with gear during the night, go down the alley instead of through the front door and sneak around to avoid them. However, they caught me with a holdall, arrested me and raided my house. All they could get me for was one bottle of counterfeit Chanel No. 5. If they'd have come the following day, when my next delivery was due, the spare bedroom would have been full to bursting point. They were really after the main man, Tommy, but he never kept gear in his house. He was safe. So was I. In fact, I was invincible. I was successful. I could get away with anything … until the day I stepped off the bus straight into the glare of police headlights. I was surrounded. I ran down an alley and hid behind a wall.

'We know you're there! You might as well come out,' they shouted.

There was no escape. I stood up and said: 'I'm only looking for something I threw over the wall last night.'

They took my holdall containing the fakes and the £200 I'd just picked up. I got four years for theft, handling stolen goods, selling counterfeit gear, affray and police assault. I was twenty years old and already facing prison for the third time. But something else was about to happen, something much worse that caused me to lose all hope and sent me on a dangerous downward spiral.

1. Borstals were prisons established to reform delinquent boys aged sixteen to twenty-one. They were characterised by strict discipline and corporal punishment – birching, canes and heavy leather straps. They were abolished by the Criminal Justice Act in 1982.

CHAPTER SIX

OVER THE EDGE

It wasn't much of a disco; a guy with a turntable and a few flashing lights in a rough Middlesbrough pub. But he played our music – Madness, The Specials, Selector, Bad Manners and The Angelic Upstarts. Skinheads and punks shuffled round the dance floor, shoulder to shoulder. And there, bang in the middle, giving it plenty, were my nana and Auntie Phyllis!

The skinhead disco at the Eagle pub: my nana loved it. Before I switched allegiance to the Frontline, I took her every week and once she'd had a few Carlsberg Special Brews, she'd be up having a jig with the rest of them. None of my mates took their nanas in, but they all knew her and loved her, particularly because she was so vulnerable.

I'd always had a good relationship with my nana; she was great fun and I thought the world of her. In later years, after I'd given up being a skinhead, I visited her every week at my mam's hotel and we'd often talk for hours. My mam had given her a job in the hotel kitchens. It was the first time she'd ever worked and she loved it. She had a purpose and she made friends. She looked so well; for those few years, she was the best I'd ever seen her.

One night she finished work at about 11pm and had a

few Carlsberg Special Brews, before I walked her back to the cottage. She was getting a bit tired by then. We got to the door and I said goodnight and gave her a kiss.

'Goodnight, God bless, I love you,' she replied.

As I walked away, she shouted after me: 'You know I love you, don't you?' I thought it was a bit strange. I went to my room in the hotel.

*   *   *   *   *

'Gram, wake up. You've got to come to the cottage – *now*!'

My stepdad was banging on the door. I jumped out of bed in a panic. What had happened? Was it my mam – had something happened to her? Was it the police again?

I got dressed really quickly, but part of me didn't want to go. I couldn't face what was there in case it was too awful. I was tempted to swig some vodka to drown the awful feelings of fear and panic.

I ran to the cottage and found my mam in tears. It was my nana. She'd suffered a fatal heart attack. I ran inside and found her slumped on the toilet, completely still. I went into shock and started banging my head against the wall. I felt so helpless. I couldn't do anything. I couldn't go near her, because the police and ambulance had been called.

I wouldn't let the ambulance crew take her. My mam pleaded with me to let them past and eventually I gave in. But I had to get away. I left the hotel and went back to Middlesbrough. I still couldn't believe she was gone; I thought she was still in the hotel. But then something else happened; I had a phone call from Durham police saying they wanted to talk to me. As soon as I arrived at the station, the memories came flooding back.

'We're going to get you for murder, so you might as well tell us the truth!'

'You're a liar. You did it!'

Three years previously I'd been locked up in those cells when that lad had been killed by a bus. But this was much worse. This was an accusation against someone I loved. My nana's purse had gone missing and I was the main suspect.

'Did you leave the latch off the cottage, then?' one copper asked me. 'Did you try to get in to take her money? We know you're a thief. Is that what happened? Did you scare her to death?'

The rage and the hurt I felt was indescribable. My nana had just died and now they were accusing me of having a part in her death.

'I better go before I do any damage,' I said.

'We'll just hold you for longer then,' they threatened.

'Are you holding me now?'

They said no. I stormed out without another word.

I think the seed of my alcoholism was sown that day. I bought a bottle of Olde English Cider and sat on the side of the road drinking it. 'What are you doing?' I thought. 'You're a smart lad, sat on the side of the road like a tramp. Think of your image …

So I did. I nicked a Lacoste jumper and had my hair done. I had to make myself look good. I had a reputation to protect and another mask to wear. I returned to Middlesbrough in a boiling rage and I ended up in one of the pubs. Someone was staring at me. I didn't bother to ask him why; I just walked over and punched him.

*   *   *   *   *

'Is my nana there?'

I'd woken up at Angela's house the next morning and was soon on the phone to the hotel.

I wasn't going to let it be real. It couldn't possibly be real.

My nana was fifty-six when she died, the same age my granddad was when he died ... and the same age that my dad was when he died nearly twenty years later. The funeral was very surreal. I was broken; if there was anyone I'd tried to behave for, it was her. Now she was gone. My life went downhill big-time after that day. I started drinking heavily and taking more drugs. I still wasn't into drugs that much; I snorted a few lines of cocaine occasionally and took speed to keep me awake at matches, but now it was getting more frequent. I didn't care any more.

A few weeks after she died, I was back in Deerbolt, serving four years for theft, handling stolen goods and selling counterfeit gear. Five months later I was transferred to Durham Prison. It was 1985, three days before my twenty-first birthday. Driving through the night my stomach was turning over. I was a new fish in 'the big house' and had no idea what to expect.

I was booked into reception and had my dinner in one of the large cages reserved for remand, new sentences and sex offenders. We had showers, were squirted with powder (to kill lice) and given our uniforms – if you could call them that. Once I got to know the store lads I got better clothes, but this night, I was given massive Y-fronts that needed braces to keep them up, jeans that were too tight and plastic shoes that didn't fit. Not quite the designer gear I was used to.

I was taken to my cell. Everything smelt really bad and I sat there thinking what a mess it all was. I spent most of the night asking my cell-mate about the jail. I didn't want to stand out as a newcomer the next day; it was a weakness that lads would prey on.

The next morning I stepped out of my cell into absolute chaos. I couldn't believe what I was seeing. Previously, I'd been used to dorms of eight; now I was on D wing with 900 men who'd committed every offence from shoplifting to murder.

Durham was a slop-out jail. In Deerbolt, each dorm had a toilet outside and bedpans at night. Now all we had was one green bucket for two or three men in each cell. On each landing was a large basin with an oversized plug hole in the middle to empty our buckets down. But with one basin for every 300 men, they ended up full to overflowing. The contents dripped over each of the three landings onto the floor below, and everyone in prison seemed to have either constipation or diarrhoea. I stepped over the puddles and went to the servery to get my breakfast; it was surrounded by pools of pooh and wee. The amount of people, noise and stench was unbelievable.

We were only allowed one shower a week. Surprisingly, inmates got used to the smell, but other people didn't. When Angela visited me she could smell it on my clothes. I couldn't smell anything. I thought they were really clean.

At night, all you could hear as the guard walked around was: crunch, crunch, crunch. Cockroaches – the jail was full of them. But these were about five inches long and rock hard; I threw one once and it hit the wall, landed on the floor and ran off. They were made of steel! You could hear them at night scratching, climbing through the air vent, sometimes even falling onto my pillow.

Despite the conditions, one of the worst things about this sentence was that I was grieving for my nana. Previously, she'd always been there and, even if I felt I had no one, I knew I could always go and talk my nana round. But now she wasn't there any more. I was trapped; I couldn't just walk out the door to try and escape these feelings of sorrow and loss and I couldn't get drunk to blank it all out. I had nearly two years of this. I buried it, put on another mask and got on with things.

*　　*　　*　　*　　*

'Mam, I'm out of prison. I'm going to get myself sorted this time. I need your help. Please can you help me?'

She'd heard it so many times before, but still she believed me; she wanted the best for me at the end of the day. I'd served twenty-two months of my four-year sentence and was twenty-two when I got out, but she offered to put on a belated twenty-first birthday party for me at a local pub. It was a great night, even though I was drunk for most of it. I was getting into Michael Jackson now; I'd gone from skinhead music, like Madness and Bad Manners, to George Benson and Luther Vandross with the Frontline and now it was Michael. I was 6ft5 now and trying to dress like him. I was slowly losing the plot!

We went to a nightclub after my party and I was like a new pin: designer sunglasses, pink shirt, leather jacket and long hair at the back. The DJ knew it was my birthday and played a Michael Jackson song. I decided to make an entrance on the dance floor and show off my body popping – I'd got two black lads in Deerbolt to teach me.

I had it all planned. I'd jump over the barrier, do the splits, a bit of a spin and get boogying. But it all went wrong; my foot got caught on the barrier, my sunglasses flew off, my leather jacket ended up over my head and I landed flat on my face in the middle of the dance floor! I got up and started dancing as if nothing had happened.

The day after, I collected some silver platters from the pub belonging to my mam's hotel. I stole a bottle of whisky from the bar and drank the lot. I think this was the last straw for my mam; she'd made a big effort to organise the party and she got the blame for the stolen whisky.

The drink was really taking hold now. I drank on the train travelling to matches and was more concerned about downing a few pints of cider, than mooching (looking for things to steal), stealing or fighting.

Once me and my mates were in a pub, when a fight started outside. I drank my pint so fast that when I ran out I got this massive stomach pain and threw up at the side of the road. It happened a lot after that; I'd be so greedy to finish my drink that I'd make myself ill. It wasn't long before I started to pull back from matches; I wanted to drink rather than fight.

I soon found another way of making money while drinking. I sat in a pub, usually the Masham, in Middlesbrough – I'd been going there since I was thirteen – and took orders from my 'customers'. I then went mooching round shops and nicking with my 'shopping list'. Sometimes I'd 'earn' up to £400 a day. But soon it was time for another fresh start. It was 1986 by now and I was off to London to get a job – again! I met up with some mates in a pub in West Kensington, visiting about nine pubs on the way. This time I had my escape route planned; I'd found out the bus location and times. I was ready to fail.

We were sitting having a laugh in the pub and planning to go clubbing at the weekend. My mates' boss was there and he even agreed to give me a sub before starting the job. I bought everyone a drink, went to the toilet ... and disappeared. While they were sat wondering where I'd gone, I was on the overnight bus home. Another failed attempt at a new start.

I didn't sleep at my house much and it was an absolute mess. I flitted between friends' houses like Santa, turning up at all hours with loads of nicked stuff. I'd fill carrier bags and walk out of supermarkets. Sometimes I took other people's shopping or takeaways. That was a surprise; I didn't know what I was getting until I opened them.

But it always caught up with me in the end. One day the police found me and my mates sitting in a field drowning our sorrows with packs of lager; our latest break-in had been a disaster. We'd got into a beer and wine warehouse, expecting to have a brilliant party. But there was no beer, wine or spirits, only hundreds of bottles of soft drinks. We'd burgled a lemonade factory! I'd already been charged with shoplifting and assault on an opposing fan and here was another thing to add to the list. I was back in Durham Prison.

Fourteen months later I was out and looking forward to going home. I arrived and tried to open my front door with the key, but it wouldn't work. I knocked on the door and it was opened by someone I'd never seen before.

'Who are you?' he said.

'What are you on about? This is my house.'

'No it's not. It's mine. I bought it off the estate agents. Quick sale.'

I was shocked. I had no idea. I knew my house had been badly damaged; the police had raided it and not had it boarded up. All my possessions had been stolen, including photos of my nana. But I never found out how I'd lost my house. I had no proof that it had been bought for me with some of the money from my granddad's will.

Angela had finally given up on me and got engaged to someone else. I was really cut up about that. My life was in pieces; a few years previously I'd had money, my own home, a girlfriend, possessions, status and power. Now I'd lost my nana, my house, my girlfriend, all my money, and my mam had finally disowned me. And there was nothing I could do about it. Nothing, that is, apart from another moneymaking scam. I'd learned this one in jail: credit card fraud. If the local moochers found a purse or wallet, me and my mate, Chrissy, would buy the credit card from them and use it round the country. It was easy money. We bought goods, paid for them, got £50 cash back each time and sold the gear in pubs. We were knocking off up to £3,000 a day until we got caught.

FROM LEFT:
Paul, Uncle Terry, Grandad, Nana, Mam and me, on holiday at Pontins

Nana and me at Bambrough Castle

At Smiggy's house, getting ready before going down the 'Boro for a fight

Maca and me, chilling out, waiting for the pub to open, 1980

Ayresome Park, MFC where I went to football most Saturdays between the ages of 8 and 28

Me at Scarborough when we went to fight the mods, 1979

My medical card certifying I'm partially sighted. They won't accept my restored sight is a miracle so they've refused to take it back.

Middlesbrough
Borough Council

SOCIAL SERVICES DEPARTMENT
REGISTRATION AS VISUALLY IMPAIRED

This is to certify that

mr Graham seed

of **21 Agecroft Gardens middlesbrough**

is registered as a Partially Sighted Person.

Team Manager Sensory Loss Service

(Signature of Issuing Officer)

28.7.97 (Date)

THIS CERTIFICATE IS SPECIFICALLY FOR
THE USE OF THE PERSON NAMED ABOVE

This certificate is issued persuant to section 29 of the National
Assistance Act 1948 and has no significance in relation to the
Disabled persons (Employment) Acts.

IN THE COUNTY OF CLEVELAND

MEMORANDUM OF CONVICTION / ORDER / ADJUDICATION E
OF THE TEESSIDE MAGISTRATES COURT SITTING AT

Date ..29 November 1985..   Case number ....

Name of informant Or complainant	Name of defendant Age if known	Nature of offence of matter of complaint	Date of offence Or Matter of complaint
Chief Constable Police HQ PO Box 70 Ladgate Lane Middlesbrough Cleveland Represented by P.C. David Arnott P.. Mcgreavy	Seed, Graham 16 High Bank Road Ormesby Middlesbrough Cleveland D.o.b 28/4/64 Represented by Brown and Beir Defence Barrister T.A. Sinclair	In Middlesbrough Train Station, did cause GBH (section 20, Common Assault, Section 47) on rival unnamed IPs (for legal reasons, Queens Evidence) Also did cause an affray (public order act 1968) on Albert #Road Middlesbrough.	29/Nov/1985

Dated ...06 June 2006.   GBH report

Me, Martin Ruddock and Peter Conroy, at the Oakwood Centre, 29 June 1997, at my baptism

Me and the Teen Challenge students of 2001

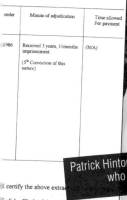

Patrick Hinton who became like a spiritual dad to me, who I really grew to love and still sadly miss.

Me, Tony and Hayley, 22 Dec 1998, taking Natasha to the train station

Me and Natasha in our back garden

Me, Natasha, Caleb and Boaz, at Flamingoland, 2007

These are the happiest days of my life, especially with my family.

But all the money in the world can't help you if you're being attacked by Freddy Krueger. He'd been following me. He was out to get me, I just knew it. He wasn't a character in a horror film any more. He was real. My head was going, slowly but surely. Me and my friend Billy, someone I'd met at the slaughterhouse, had been watching *A Nightmare on Elm Street* and its sequels, over and over again. It had poisoned my mind. I couldn't cope.

I was staying in a hostel on Wellington Street at the time and a couple of the staff members, Big Ian and Fiona, became friends. I told them my head was all over the place and they offered to help. They said they were spiritualists. I jumped at the chance, not realising that what they were about to do would affect me for the next nine years of my life.

That night, I found myself lying on their living room floor, in the dark, with candles on my arms and forehead, while they chanted round me in a weird language. I must have passed out because the next thing I knew, I'd woken up with a sheet over me. All my clothes had gone. I had no idea what had just happened and they gave me no explanation.

Later, as I slept in their house, a really heavy feeling came on me, like a huge, unbearable depression. I ran up to the windows and smashed my fists through the glass because I thought someone was standing there. I attacked the doors and walls. I had to get out.

After that night, I started hearing voices and seeing things all the time. I saw evil figures down back alleys and sometimes they would follow me. I'd try to attack them, run into doors and walls and end up covered in cuts and scratches. I thought it was the drink and drugs, but I know now it was something supernatural that I didn't understand. I'd dabbled in the occult a few times over the years; I used to visit haunted places and had done a few Ouija boards.

Angela had done one once that spelt my name. In another session someone had seen me walking past the window. I was in prison at the time ...

Whatever came on me in that room, I walked with for the next nine years; it stole my life, destroyed everything around me and tried to kill me. Since my nana had died, I'd been in a vulnerable and dangerous state and was an open target for evil.

I got kicked out of that hostel for nicking all the pictures and selling them. As I left, a big Mercedes 500 SEL rolled up and a smart-looking guy got out. He asked if I worked there and I said yes (just in case it was going to be helpful for me). He'd brought eighteen Italian suits for the lads in the hostel, which he'd had dry-cleaned. I took them from him and, when he'd gone, I ran the other way and sold them within an hour at a nearby pub.

It was nearly Christmas 1987 and I was about to go to prison again for fraud. My solicitor persuaded the court to try something different. Prison hadn't worked, he argued, but something needed to be done to help me. So they sent me to St Luke's, where my nana had been a day patient. Even though I remembered what they'd done to her, it was a relief to go there; I wanted to find out what was wrong with me and to stop drinking.

The first couple of days were horrific. They were trying to poison me, I was convinced of it. I refused to drink or eat anything. I had horrible visions: giant spiders came at me; doors opened by themselves and people stood there staring at me; a huge guy with massive fingers and four arms hovered over my bed. I tried to fight him off; I was sweating and shouting and the next day I was absolutely drained, like a zombie. I thought at the time it was withdrawal symptoms from the drink.

I was diagnosed with manic depression and placed in the Bristol ward, for those who'd had breakdowns, and alcohol and drug problems. There were some really sad cases; one guy thought he was an egg, another believed he was Elvis. After a week though, I was a different character; I hadn't had a drink for seven days, I was clean, shaved and feeling pretty fit. I started running the place – picking the videos, TV programmes and having a laugh with them all. It ended up being a great Christmas. I finally felt safe.

After three weeks I was told that I would be assessed and would probably be considered fit enough to leave. I panicked; I wanted to stay in this make-believe bubble. I couldn't face what was out there again.

'I can't leave. I'm not well and I'm dangerous,' I pleaded with them.

'You'll have to go. This isn't a hotel, you know,' I was told.

The night before I was due to leave, I couldn't sleep. I booked a taxi to pick me up at 4pm, but when the driver arrived, I ran back inside and hid. I came out when he'd gone and sat on a nearby bench until 11pm that night. I tried to get back into the ward, claiming I'd left something there.

'I'm not leaving. This is where I live,' I told them.

They called the police. I was escorted to the main road. I walked to the nearest shops, bought half a bottle of vodka and a bottle of orangeade, mixed them together and drank the lot. I then went to a nightclub called Rumours, saw lots of old friends and booked into a bed and breakfast.

I heard that Middlesbrough was playing a few days later, so I decided to go back to football matches. It was cold and dark as I walked to the grounds wearing steel-cap boots, shorts and a T-shirt. I started to think that I didn't really want to do this any more. But I never got there. The police spotted me, bundled me into a van and took me to Middlesbrough town centre. They told me to keep away from the match and the surrounding area that day, or I would be arrested. My bed and breakfast was in that area. I couldn't go back to it, so I wandered round on my own the rest of the night.

I was drinking earlier in the day now. I was in the Rosebury pub once when a man came in with a two-litre bottle of whisky. He asked if anyone wanted to join him. I jumped at the chance. He challenged me to a competition; three glasses of whisky followed by a pint of cider. He ended up that drunk that he wet himself. I was still feeling OK; I guess I won that one. But as soon as I left the pub, the fresh air hit me. I staggered all over the place and ended up in the driver's seat of an unattended minibus. I tried to drive it away, but I couldn't get it into gear. I gave up, wandered to a nearby bank and sat down. Meanwhile the driver had called the police and I got charged with aggravated taking without the owner's legal consent, with intent to endanger lives, drunk driving, no licence, no insurance – about nine charges altogether. I was bailed and went to stay with a family I knew, the Wards, in the Whinney Banks district … after nicking money from the B and B I'd been staying at.

It wasn't long before I got in trouble at another match. I assaulted both a fan and a policeman. I was remanded, but all the recent convictions meant that I was facing another sentence in Durham Prison, three and a half years this time. I appealed, saying my head was gone. I lost the appeal.

It was 1988 by now and this time I was very rebellious. I'd kicked off a few times in other prisons, but now I was much worse. I poured hot drinks on people's heads, swore at the officers, smashed up the cell, and then realised I'd have to live in the mess. I threw my food all over the floor once because it was so disgusting. I often got dragged, kicking and screaming to solitary – a bleak and cold room with nothing but a Bible in it. I ripped the pages out and made roll-ups from them.

*　　*　　*　　*　　*

'I'm coming home, I've done my time!' I was singing at the top of my voice on the bus back to Middlesbrough. I was free and I was buzzing with it. I was back with Angela again by now and was on my way to surprise her. Or so I thought. As soon as I got off the bus, I was surrounded by the police. I knew why.

When I left the prison that day, I'd bought some cigarettes, a newspaper and a Marathon bar from a nearby shop. When the assistant disappeared to get some change, I'd reached over and grabbed a handful of money out of the till. I just couldn't help myself. He called the police, who took the description and checked that day's releases from Durham. I was fast-tracked through the courts and sent back to Durham that day. I'd been boasting to one of the officers that morning with my 'prison talk', saying how I was going to sort myself out and I'd never be back in here again. His eyes nearly popped out of his head when he saw me. He hadn't even finished his shift!

The following week, after serving twenty-two months of my three-and-a-half year sentence – plus an extra seven days – I was out. I didn't really know what to do with myself. Old friends were doing other stuff and the police were clamping down on match violence in a big way. It wasn't the same any more.

I was still stealing, but I was barred from Middlesbrough town centre. I didn't know where to go. I managed to get caught for drink driving twice; during one arrest, I pushed the police officer and he took a dive over the bonnet. Suddenly I was surrounded by coppers.

I did a bit of credit card fraud again, but I had a feeling the guy I was helping was 'bent' (a police informant). Then almost by accident, I came across another moneymaking scheme. There was a car outside a pub one night and one of the hub caps was missing. I told the owner I could get some for him for £15. They would have cost him about £38 for a new set. Soon I was selling up to forty sets a week. I was back at football matches, nicking instead of fighting. With hundreds of unattended cars outside the grounds, I could easily get thirty sets in my boot within an hour.

One day one of my 'customers' asked for some Mercedes hub caps. I did my research and had a chat with him over a game of pool and a few pints. I walked out the pub and straight away spotted a nearby Mercedes. It had clips on the hub caps, so I took out my Stanley knife and cut the clips off. The next minute, I was surrounded. My 'customer' was an undercover policeman.

I was now convicted of five accounts of theft, two accounts of drink driving and common assault on a policeman. I was back in Durham Prison. This time, a lot of my friends weren't around and I was very depressed. However, I decided that I'd had enough of crime. I had a plan – Gram's grand plan that would guarantee me success. I spent all my time thinking about it. It couldn't possibly go wrong; this was what I'd waited for all my life. I'd decided to move away, get out of Middlesbrough and find a job. I knew a family in Scissett, near Wakefield that I could stay with until I found a flat. I was excited and hopeful. It was an awesome, foolproof plan.

I got out on 20 July 1990 and spent my last month in Middlesbrough at a probation hostel. I packed up, said goodbye to my friends and left. I was twenty-six and about to start my new life. I wasn't going to fail this time.

*   *   *   *   *

There was a stranger in the village, and the villagers were worried. A very tall, sinister-looking guy, in denim jeans and jacket, covered in tattoos, had been seen acting suspiciously. I'd arrived in Scissett! All I'd done was walk to the house where I was staying. By the time I'd arrived, the woman who ran the Neighbourhood Watch for the area had received ten calls about me.

'Get a flat quickly,' she told me.

I was determined this time that I wasn't going to get into trouble. I'd brought my new girlfriend, Karen, from Middlesbrough and we rented a flat together. I got a job cutting up and moving boxes at a catalogue firm on the outskirts of Wakefield. I was claiming dole, so I was still a con merchant, but I did my job well and socialised with work colleagues. I was finally respectable.

But soon we started running out of money. I looked for something to steal. That year the catalogue firm were offering 'his and hers' watches for those who placed orders. I knew where the cupboard was and every day I transferred at least eleven sets into a sack and hid them in my bag. I sold them in Wakefield pubs; I think everyone in Wakefield had 'his and hers' watches that Christmas.

One day, the security guard stopped me and searched my bag.

'Who put them there?' I said when he found the watches. 'You want rid of me, don't you? Have you found out I'm a jailbird? I'm trying to sort myself out. Why would I want to do anything like that?'

The boss said he wouldn't call the police, but asked me to leave.

I went back to working on the doors. I'd done it occasionally since I was sixteen, usually when pubs and clubs I went in needed someone at short notice. Being a bouncer was easy money and a good way to impress girls. I got a job at the Woolpack in Wakefield. The boss offered me £35 a night, for five nights, to work the alley doorway – the rough part where there were drugs and beatings.

I was always flirting with one of the barmaids. One night, I followed her downstairs and we had sex in the cellar. We got together a few times after that, but then I told her to leave me alone. She told my boss I was selling drugs and he gave me £100 to get rid of me.

My next job was at the Dolphin for £38 a night … £3 more. I was going up in the world! The boss, Rick, had connections with a local nightclub, the Rooftop Gardens and he got me a job working there each night when the Dolphin closed. I was then getting £50 from the nightclub and I was still claiming the dole and stealing. I was doing all right now, so surely I was allowed to nick the odd jumper?

Karen had got fed up with me cheating on her and getting drunk, so she went back to Middlesbrough. By Christmas she decided to give me another chance. We planned a big party on New Year's Eve at our flat, after I'd finished in the club that night. But I never made it.

That evening we were told to shut the doors just before midnight, but the girls on the cash desk closed them too early. A couple of fights broke out; we were throwing some lads out and as I came back in, someone suddenly ran at us; he had something in his hand that looked like a bottle. I thought he was going to hit another bouncer, so I punched him, threw him out and locked the doors.

We had just celebrated New Year with champagne and poppers when the police arrived. A guy pointed to me – I didn't have a clue who he was at this point – and I was bundled into a police van. I'd always resisted arrest until then, but this time I didn't struggle. It was 12.45am. They didn't interview me until 9am the next day.

'What's this all about? You got a warrant from Middlesbrough?' I said.

'That man who pointed you out said you hit him,' I was told.

'I hit a few people that night.'

'He was an undercover policeman.'

As they talked through the details, I remembered who they meant – the guy with the bottle at the end of the night. I wasn't having any of it.

'He can't have been undercover – he was drunk. Where is he, then? Why is he not here, dealing with this? Is he somewhere sobering up?'

Usually, someone who's undercover will deal with the case and the paperwork that night. They said he was having an X-ray on his jaw, but I knew I'd hit him on the back of the head; I had a mark on my knuckle. He even later claimed that it was a walkie-talkie in his hand, not a bottle. Not very undercover, then!

My girlfriend had left me again when I didn't turn up for the party; it was the last straw for her.

I pleaded not guilty, but I still got thirteen months in Leeds Prison. As far as I was concerned, that was the end; there was nothing left to live for. I'd tried so hard to change, to make a fresh start, to put my past behind me. I'd failed. My awesome, foolproof, grand plan was in tatters.

I'd never been so low. I didn't talk to anyone, even though I knew a lot of the lads from other prisons, I didn't go to the gym and spent most of my time alone in my cell. I was drained, defeated, like a zombie, and desperate for a drink.

When I got out in 1992, after serving thirteen months, I visited my old boss, Rick, at the Dolphin. He'd sold some of my property from the flat for me and I went to collect the money. He'd put some extra money aside; he felt really guilty about that night because he'd got me the nightclub job and I'd done nothing wrong. I was just doing my job.

I was soon on the train back to Middlesbrough. I'd phoned some old mates to let them know what time I was arriving. I was excited. I was going home! I couldn't wait to see everyone at the station. I don't quite know what I expected – a band, crowds cheering and waving banners, the mayor! There had to be something, someone to welcome me, surely.

My welcome party didn't exist. I got off the train and there was no one there to meet me. Feeling alone and miserable, I decided to try a few old haunts like Chaplains and Trouper. Everything had changed and I didn't recognise anyone. One of the landlords glanced at me as I came in.

'Oh hi, Gram, I haven't seen you for a while,' he said and carried on with his conversation. I hadn't been there since 1989! Where were the party and the free drinks?

It was Christmas and the decorations and lights were everywhere. I was getting more and more depressed as I wandered round on my own, not knowing where to go or what to do. What had happened to my town, my mates, my life?

And then I found it: the place where I could finally be myself, stop pretending and feel safe. It was a place where I was about to spend the next three years of my life, until the day I left, wrapped in a 'body bag', cold, lifeless, and as good as dead.

CHAPTER SEVEN

WHEN ALL HOPE IS GONE

It was just an ordinary bench. Nothing special. It had no shelter, no nice view – just a post office and a few shops. Nobody went there, except the local drug addicts and prostitutes. It was bang in the middle of Middlesbrough's red light district. It had little to attract anyone. But it attracted me. I lived there. It was my bench, my home. My place to die.

Wandering round that night I spotted some lads sat drinking, playing music and having a laugh. I joined them and suddenly I felt young again. At this point I was fitter and smarter than they were – they were all addicts – but I also found that all the pressure was off and I didn't have to try and impress anyone. I could let it all go.

I sat with them every night after that. It was such a relief not having to try, as I'd done for so many years. I'd spent hours in the gym and on the sunbed, followed the crew, worn the right clothes and the right trainers, went to the right clubs. I always had to be the best; surely that was the only way to find love and get friends? But sitting on that bench, I didn't have to try and be somebody. I could finally be nobody. All the masks were starting to fall off. I didn't need them any more.

But I still thought I should have a proper home. I rented a flat in the council estate overlooking the bench, on Grange

Road, but hardly used it. The only furniture was a bed in the front room. I started renting it to the local prostitutes, so they didn't have to use cars or alleyways. I used the money for drink.

That first year on the bench, I started to deteriorate. I'd stopped training in the gym, drank most of the time and didn't eat much, so I started losing weight. I sometimes stayed with friends or girlfriends, or hung around in the local pub and slept by the fire. I'd wake up, run my head under the tap – I'd shaved my hair off to save money on haircuts – and go out on the town. If I thought I was going to pull, I went into Boots and sprayed myself with tester aftershaves. I still stole clothes, but mainly from charity shops. Even my nicking had gone downmarket. But my stealing soon caught up with me again and I found myself doing three months in Holme House Prison, Stockton.

Holme House was known locally as 'Holme from Home' because it was so close to Middlesbrough. It was really posh; it had a toilet and washbasin in the cell, a really good gym, and association (let out onto the wing for socialising) from day one.

When I first arrived, an officer said to me, 'I'll be along in a minute with the menu.'

I scoffed at him and called him a load of names. I thought he was having a laugh. My experiences of prison food up to then had been pretty awful. At Deerbolt it was boiled away to nothing, with no goodness. The meat was processed and hard and the custard was like water with lumps in. Durham dinners were served in shallow trays with little compartments; by the time you had walked back to your cell, they had overflowed into each other and your dinner and pudding ended up mixed together. The potatoes always had black bits in them and you often found unidentified objects in the rest. Medomsley's food was virtually non-existent. That was part of the punishment: no sweets, plain, awful food and not much of it. I was expecting more of the same.

The officer came back with a bit of paper and I said, 'D'you think I'm daft or something? Get out of here before I ask to see the governor.'

'Fine,' he said. 'Don't eat.'

My cell-mate came in and I said, 'What's all this about a menu?'

He said it was true.

'What is this? Butlins or something?' I said in disbelief.

I was given diazepam to help with the withdrawal from alcohol, but I didn't like the effect; it made me really tired. I used to hide the tablets under my false teeth (some of my real ones were knocked out through fighting) and, when the guard had gone, I would sell them for extra phone credit and cannabis.

As soon as I got out, I was back on my bench. I was a chronic alcoholic by now. The drink got rid of the hallucinations and dark thoughts that had haunted me for years: everything I'd done and everything I had been. That bench to me was my escape; I could sit drinking all day and have no thoughts, pain, guilt or shame.

I begged for money from passers-by, borrowed from friends and nicked from phone boxes. Once I asked a pub doorman if they'd have a whip-round for me. I felt so embarrassed and humiliated, but I had to drink. I even tried to save £10 once to buy a new jumper, but I spent it on drink.

By Christmas 1993 I'd reached my lowest point. Everyone around me was doing what I used to do – buying decorations and presents and visiting friends and family. I tried to drown out the memories with drink, but it wasn't working any more; it wasn't touching the parts it was supposed to. All the dark thoughts came flooding back. I couldn't take it any more. I had no hope. At 3am one morning I took a knife from down my sock and slit my wrists.

I managed to gouge my left arm open and tried to cut the other one, but the knife stuck in my hand. I collapsed and was found unconscious by the police.

They thought someone had tried to murder me.

'Who did this? We couldn't find anyone to talk to about you,' I was asked the next day in hospital.

'Nobody. I did it to myself.'

They had no one to ask – no one who could identify me or tell them about me. That got to me – I really was completely alone. I had to get out. I needed a drink. I pulled the drip out of my arm, put on my bloodstained clothes and left. I ate a big piece of black pudding on the way back to my bench. I'd heard that it put the blood back in your system.

By the time 1994 arrived, I was getting physically weaker and I couldn't be bothered to look after myself. I had the occasional cold bath in the flat – the gas and electric had been cut off because I hadn't paid the bills – or a shower in the local swimming baths. I'd lost my touch with girls. All my nice clothes and jewellery had long since disappeared. I was scruffy and smelt bad. But all I cared about was drinking.

I realised how weak I'd got when I was attacked a couple of times and couldn't fight back. I tried to hit someone once when he insulted me, but couldn't defend myself when he hit me back. I'd always been a fighter and able to stick up for myself. Now I couldn't even do that any more

Another time, one of the lads I was drinking with was attacked with a baseball bat. I got up to help and the attacker pushed me down and slapped me. I tried again. He hit me again. Now I couldn't stick up for my friend either. Surely if I couldn't help him, he wouldn't like me any more. I had nothing to offer him.

Deep down I didn't really want to be like this. I tried rehab once, in an old army camp on Chester-Lee Street. I went through all the admissions procedures, took one look at my bed and the other people in there, and fled to the nearest off-licence. I couldn't do it.

My friends Mike Maloney and Lizzie Ward tried to get me back into St Luke's. It took them all day to get me admitted but as soon I was in, being without a drink was too unbearable. I kicked the fire exit open and ran out.

An old friend of mine, Tony, found me one day and couldn't believe what he saw; this once smart lad lying unconscious on the pavement like a tramp. He took me home, gave me a bath and some clean clothes. His wife burned my old ones. However, the next day I was so desperate to get a drink that I ran out of the house wearing nothing except a pair of boxer shorts. But I was too ill to get very far; everything started closing in on me. So I stumbled back indoors and sat down. I didn't move from that chair for three weeks. The last straw for Tony came when I got drunk, smashed a large jardinière and tried to blame the dog. He told me he loved me, but I would have to leave. He couldn't help me any more.

*   *   *   *   *

'You can take the handcuffs off him now,' said the doctor.

'We already have.'

I was in casualty with the police. My arms were dangling helplessly by my sides. I couldn't move them. I'd been arrested for aggravated shoplifting, after elbowing a security guard. The police had chased me and dragged me along the ground, pulling my arms out of their sockets. They were pushed painfully back into place and I was bailed. But I knew I couldn't face another Christmas in jail. How would I cope without a drink? I knew I'd have to go on the run.

I smartened myself up and went to a local nightclub with Tony. I asked someone to dance. She was called Susan and she'd seen me years ago and had wanted to go out with me then. She was from Stokesley, about fifteen miles away. Stokesley, I thought. That would be a good place to hide!

I took her to my cesspool of a flat. It stank and there were condoms everywhere; Durham jail was cleaner! Afterwards, she gave me her phone number. I rang the next day and she asked me to come to her house.

'Looks like I'm here for Christmas,' I told Tony as he dropped me off.

It was a lovely area. Stokesley's council estates were better than Middlesbrough's private estates. Susan also had a garden shed packed full of foreign beer and lager; she used to sell it. I thought I was in heaven. I had somewhere to live and a shed full of beer! I couldn't give this place up.

'I'm going to jail soon. Are you going to come and visit me?' I asked her, casually, one day.

'What! Jail? You can't go. Why not stay here with me?'

That was what I wanted to hear. 'Nah, it's all right, I don't want to be any bother.' I was good at this.

'No, stay, please,' she insisted.

'All right, but I'll only bring a few things.' I only *had* a few things!

I'd also brought my old behaviour with me. That Christmas I stole from local shops and sold stuff in pubs; I got barred out of every pub in the area because I was loud and aggressive. I even stole from Susan's boss's house. I didn't care, especially once Christmas was over. I started going back to Middlesbrough and staying out all night.

Susan was getting really fed up by now. One day she asked me to collect some wallpaper from Middlesbrough that she'd already paid for. I got a refund from the shop – it was nearly £200 – and spent it all on drink. I tried to lie to her about it when I got back, but she'd already phoned the shop. She also accused me of sleeping with someone else. I opened a can of beer and sat watching TV, trying to ignore her shouts and accusations. Finally, I'd had enough.

'Yes I did sleep with her, in your bed, and she was much better than you!' I yelled back.

She disappeared into the kitchen for ages, came back and kicked the glass panel on the door, cutting her toe badly.

'Look, you've got blood all over the carpet now.' I showed no concern for her.

She disappeared again and came back with a big knife. 'I'm going to kill you,' she yelled. 'I can't take any more. You've done my head in for months. You've got me a bad name in the area – I can't even walk through town any more – and now you're sleeping with other girls!'

I thought she was joking. I was sitting on her leather settee; she was really fussy about it and wouldn't even let me sit on it with jeans. She came at me. I jumped out of the way and the knife went straight through the settee. I knew she wasn't joking then. I shot up and she came at me again. I was backed into a corner. I'd dealt with enough knife attacks and knew if I lost my balance, I'd had it. I could see the knife coming towards my heart, so I grabbed the blade. It nearly severed my little finger – it was hanging off. Susan started screaming and crying. I grabbed a tea towel, wrapped it round my hand, held it up in the air and sat watching TV. I didn't feel any pain. I just wanted to stop the blood and blank it all out.

'You're going to kill me, aren't you?' she screamed. The windows were open and by now all the neighbours were out on the street. I asked her to phone Tony to come and get me.

I heard the police siren and ran into the woods at the back of the house to meet him.

Tony tried to get me to go to hospital, but all I wanted was a fresh towel to wrap round my finger. However, I started feeling weak from losing so much blood, so finally, five hours later, I let him take me to A and E. I was rushed into the emergency theatre to try and save my finger. I stayed awake and refused any anaesthetic, but the finger was dead by now. They had to amputate it.

The police picked me up trying to get back to Stokesley. The next day I was sentenced to six months in Holme House. My hand was really painful by now and I was given no painkillers. The cell beds had horrible woollen mesh sheets that stuck to my finger. It soon got infected.

Susan visited me in prison and asked me to live with her again. But when I left and returned to her house that September, I couldn't forget what she'd done.

We were out in a pub one evening and Susan's mates were having a laugh about what had happened.

'It's a good job it was just your finger. I'd have chopped your bits off if it was me!'

I wasn't laughing.

That night I couldn't sleep; I had visions of her coming at me in bed with a knife, and this time it wasn't my finger she was after.

The next morning I told her I was going to Middlesbrough for the day and left. I never saw her again.

It wasn't long before the depression came back. Jail had perked me up and given a structure to my life; I'd had three meals a day, a clean bed to sleep in, went to the gym, I was clean and smelling nice, had half-decent clothes, fags and music. I was also off the booze. Without that structure, there was nothing to stop me returning to my old way of life.

*   *   *   *   *

I stood staring at the tramp in front of me; I couldn't believe the state he was in. His jeans were soiled and stained with muck and blood, his skin was thick with dirt and his fingernails blackened, he had vomit down his top, a filthy beard and scratches all over his bald head. He stank and looked like he hadn't eaten for months. He was in a desperate state.

He was me.

I turned away from the shop mirror and looked across to the Masham pub. Suddenly I saw myself years before, walking in wearing my Armani suit and crocodile skin shoes. I cried all the way back to my bench because I couldn't believe how far I'd fallen. I was rejected by everyone who knew me. I'd conned them all, borrowed money and not paid it back. One mate would still give me a fiver just to get me out of his shop, I smelt so bad. But even the criminal world didn't want to know me now.

But I told myself tomorrow it would all be different. I would smarten myself up, get all my old clothes back, never drink again. Every evening, when the drink had kicked in, I felt I could achieve anything. I was always going to stop drinking the next day. I made a feeble attempt to change sometimes. I even tried selling clothes again. But who would buy from a smelly tramp?

One of the last people to try and help me was my mate Andrew Smith, who I knew as Smiggy. I'd known him since I was a teenager, when I used to climb through his window in the early hours of the morning and hide under his bed to avoid his dad. He thought I was a bad influence. Once his dad was at work, I would come out and have breakfast with him.

Now he was the manager of a designer clothes shop and would sometimes give me free gear to try and tidy me up.

He also employed me to do a few odd jobs, but I even did the dirty on him and let him down. He tried his hardest and I threw it back in his face.

I was deteriorating quickly. I drank seven two-litre bottles of White Lightning cider every day. At one time, I would enjoy the taste of a pint, but not any more. This stuff was like paint stripper, burning my throat. But it was strong and I needed it just to feel normal now; the buzz I used to get from alcohol had long since disappeared.

I sat on my bench in all weathers, often in just a T-shirt; sometimes I would wake up in the morning and my T-shirt would be stiff with frost. Old enemies or kids walking by would spit at me and hit me with sticks. One time I looked in the mirror and saw I had black eyes and a bleeding mouth. Another time I was covered in scratches; I was told some lads had dragged me through some nearby privets when I was unconscious. Others put fags out on my head and threw dog pooh at me. I was too drunk to care, but the voices in my head had plenty to say about it.

'Look at the state of you. You're useless!'

'You let them do that to you? What a wimp!'

'Everyone's looking at you. They think you're a mess, a waste of space.'

I never understood where the voices were coming from, but I just tried to drown them out with drink. I'd get as much painkiller in me as quickly as possible; sometimes I'd try and get it down so fast that I'd throw it up all over myself. First thing I did when I woke up was throw up bile, before I reached for the bottle.

I made a decision not to eat; if I ate, I couldn't drink as much. However, sometimes I was so uncontrollably hungry I would be forced to find food to get rid of the hunger pains. I'd follow people with takeaways, waiting for them to be thrown away, so I could scavenge the leftovers. Sometimes I'd rummage through bins to pick bits out of empty pizza or kebab boxes. Once someone felt sorry for me and nicked money to buy me some KFC chicken. The next day I woke up in a panic, without my false teeth, thinking I'd swallowed them. I then remembered I'd put them in the KFC lid for safe-keeping – and thrown the box away.

In those three and a half years I spent on the bench, I must have been arrested about fifty times for causing trouble. I often staggered up to people intimidating them for money. I'd walk into Marks and Spencer's, open cans of wine and soda and drink them. I went into supermarkets, opened pasties or packets of cheese and started to eat them. Once I opened some coffee granules and said to a horrified shop assistant, 'I'm going to have a cup of coffee. Where's the cups?' Another time I staggered into a furniture store, sat on a settee, put my feet up and asked where the remote control was.

One day I was chatting to some lads on my bench about gardens.

'That's what we need – a garden for the bench!' I decided. I disappeared and came back with two big flower tubs on wheels and arranged them round the bench. 'Look, now we've got a garden.' I'd stolen them from outside McDonalds.

Often I was sent to court for being drunk and disorderly, for breach of the peace or for theft, but it was always dismissed because of the state I was in. I think the magistrate told the police to stop charging me, because it was a waste of money. Instead they often locked me up for the night and released me the next day without charge, to get me off the streets and sober me up.

Sometimes I wandered to different areas – I made sure I had bottles of cider hidden all over Middlesbrough – but I still couldn't escape what I was. I was like Pigpen from the

Charlie Brown comic strip – the character with all the flies buzzing round him; the one that people avoided.

Christmas Day 1995 was my worst ever. While everyone else was enjoying the festivities, I was crawling half a mile on my hands and knees to reach the off-licence; I was too ill to walk. I was freezing cold, my T-shirt was frozen stiff and my jeans were wet with wee. But I had to get there. I could get a three-litre bottle of White Lightning on the slate – this shop owner knew I'd pay him back. I had no other options. I was desperate.

Sometimes I was aware of the state I was in, but most of the time I was past caring. I was a bit more concerned on Tuesdays, when I got my dole money; I went to a nearby pub for a couple of hours to warm up and try and feel normal. Sometimes I chatted to strangers, reminiscing about my past. I made lies up about why I was in this state and told them I had a job to go to the following week. I left the pub longing for it to be true.

In 1996 my insides started shutting down. I wasn't aware of it. It was like looking in a mirror when you have a headache; you can't see your headache. My liver and kidneys were breaking down and would soon stop working. I was dying on that bench and I had no idea.

I began to lose my functions and started weeing and poohing myself, sometimes without knowing and never able to stop it. The first time it happened, I laughed about it with my mates on the bench. But soon it was happening every day and it wasn't funny any more. I waited for the charity shops to open so I could nick a pair of jeans; mine were soaking wet and mucky every morning. I left my soiled ones in the changing room.

I tried heroin in that final year. I chased the dragon (breathing in the fumes from foil) and sometimes addicts would stick needles in my arms. Surely something would happen, I thought, hopefully. But I felt nothing; it just made me feel weird and tired. I tried anything to get some kind of buzz, but the only thing that really did it for me was drink.

I'd become more of a recluse by then; the other lads who hung round the bench didn't bother with me any more. I didn't have time for anyone; I was in my own little world. I talked to myself, reminiscing about how smart I used to be and all the money and friends I'd had. I'd lost touch with my family years ago, although my mam made an effort to bring me a birthday card that April. She was a bit late, so I spat at the car and swore at her.

The previous ten years had been hell for my mam. All I ever did was pester her for money and steal from the hotel. I ransacked her cottage once, looking for money when she'd refused to give me any. I'd even told her friend and my uncle that she was dead when she'd gone on holiday. It was another attempt to get money. I was a lowlife and I didn't care who I hurt. Mam had had enough. One day she'd taken me into the cottage, got her chequebook out and said: 'How much will it take to never see you again?'

'A couple of grand,' I'd said.

'Get out!' She got an injunction banning me from the hotel and village. She'd disowned me. I didn't blame her.

I think deep down I missed my family; I often went to the cemetery where my nana and granddad's ashes were and sometimes woke up there on the ground, drunk. But it didn't stop me mistreating those who were still alive and trying to help.

*   *   *   *   *

That spring, 1996, I was cold, smelly and desperate. I had nobody and I didn't think anyone loved me. Who in their right mind would want to? I hated myself for what I'd become and there was nothing to live for any more. After my suicide attempt, I decided not to try and kill myself again because the drink would do it soon enough. I thought I might as well die 'happy' by drinking myself to death.

Then, one Friday night, some lads walked up to my bench. I'd never seen them before. One of them – I later found out he was called Brian Wade – said to me: 'Do you know that Jesus loves you?' I swore at them and told them to get lost.

They didn't give in. Brian told me his story: he used to be an alcoholic until Jesus rescued him. I thought he was off his head, worse than I was! I was also angry because he'd tried to tell me that someone loved me. Nobody loved me. I knew that. I believed the only way to get love was to find it yourself – 'nobody gives owt for nowt'.

They came back again later. They must have had some bottle! They talked to me again and they later told me I prayed with them to ask Jesus to help me; I was too drunk to remember. I saw them everywhere that week, which seemed a bit weird. The following Friday they came back and bought me a burger. I sold it to one of the prostitutes for £1.50 to get a bottle of White Lightning. This could be useful, I thought. I'll con them into giving me lifts and money.

A couple of weeks later, I fell asleep in the flat in front of the electric fire – someone had wired it up illegally to get it working. A lad visiting his prostitute girlfriend came in and found me surrounded by clouds of smoke. I'd burnt all of my leg.

*   *   *   *   *

'Gram, look at the state of your leg. What happened?'

Those Christians were back! I didn't know why they were

so concerned, but a couple of weeks later, they asked about it again. I later found out the guys' names: Mike Horner and Aiden Poulton. They tried to take me to hospital, but I refused. They came back later that night and offered again.

'Only if I can take my White Lightning,' I told them.

In hospital, with my bottle of cider hidden in a big coat, I sat on a trolley while the nurse tried to take my socks off. She suddenly stopped, stared at my feet and went to get the doctor. He told me that my socks would have to be removed with a scalpel. All the skin on the bottom of my feet appeared to have attached itself to my socks with a mixture of muck and fungus; I'd worn them for months. The nurse washed my leg with a cloth and it was black. The dirt was ground in and almost as thick as a second skin.

All that went through my mind that night was: why do these Christians want to help me so much and take me to hospital? What do they want from me? Do I owe them something that I'd forgotten about? Was I being set up? I was very wary.

But while they spent endless hours every week chatting to me, giving me lifts, showing me that they cared, offering me the only glimmer of hope in what was left of my life, I was finally losing my last bit of sanity. I'd turned into a dog. I knew I was a dog because I was on all fours, barking at and biting everyone who dared to come near my bench. But that wasn't enough. I needed more people to bite. I squeezed through a broken window pane to get into the flat – the key had long since disappeared – and attacked the prostitutes and drug addicts gathered inside, barking, growling, biting. Eventually, exhausted and desperately sick, I collapsed, unconscious, on the floor. My body had finally given in.

CHAPTER EIGHT

RESURRECTION

'I just couldn't believe the state of him. He was always such a big lad – but now there was nothing left of him. He was like a skeleton.'
Pat Lawson

I was in a beautiful room – clean, white and fresh. Two huge fans were blowing out the purest air you could ever imagine. Two women, dressed in white were moving round, constantly cleaning, constantly smiling. As I sat on the white settee watching them, they came over, dusted me down and cleaned me too. I certainly needed it.

Everything went dark and I saw myself as a wax figure. I had no neck or proper legs and I was covered with words like swearing, violence, deceit, burglary and the faces of everyone I'd hurt in the past. Suddenly, the figure was engulfed by flames and the words and faces started dripping off and disappearing. As the figure melted away, a large hand lifted me up and lowered me gently into a huge, endless pool full of the most amazingly clean and pure water.

Meanwhile, outside my head, the nurses and doctors who had been desperately trying to save me were preparing to turn off my life support. There was nothing more they could do.

'Gram's dead!' The message spread quickly round Middlesbrough the night my friends found me unconscious. Someone spotted me being carried to the ambulance in what appeared to be a body bag. In fact, I was wrapped in a large, zip-up foil blanket to raise my body temperature.

I was rushed to intensive care at South Cleveland Hospital (now the James Cook University Hospital), where I was diagnosed with hypothermia, pneumonia, septicaemia, severe malnutrition, severe dehydration and my liver was starting to shut down. I'd slipped into a coma and, five days later, my kidneys started failing, which meant my brain was starting to swell. They couldn't find the right antibiotic for the septicaemia; I had eight blood transfusions to try and flush it out, but there was no response.

My family were contacted. I later discovered my mam was reluctant to come at first, until she was told how serious it was. She was shocked when she saw the state I was in. She had both dreaded and expected this moment for years.

'I'm sorry, Mrs Lawson, but your son isn't responding to treatment. As his only legal guardian, we are advising you to allow us to switch off his life support. There's nothing more we can do for him.'

So now even the doctors had given up. But she hadn't. Despite everything I'd done and how much I'd hurt her, I was still her son. She told them: 'Look, I want you to keep trying, at least until you've got more proof that he's not responding.'

Two hours later, they came back. It wasn't good news.

'We've tried some more tests on him and he's not responding,' they said. 'There's no oxygen in his blood and it's only the machine that's keeping him breathing now. Even if he was going to wake up, he would be paralysed from the neck down.'

My mam said, 'I don't care. You fight for him. He's only thirty-two. He's too young to die. While there's breath there, keep fighting!'

A lot of people came to the hospital. Friends had rung

round everyone who knew me. Some had even left their drinks in the pub to rush down. A lot of them wanted to find out the truth. Was I really dead?

On the sixth day, the Christians, Pete Conroy, Aiden and Mike arrived. They had missed me on my bench, asked around and found out what had happened.

'Can we pray for him?' they asked my mam.

'Yes, of course. I don't know what you mean by pray for him, but go for it.'

So they laid hands on me and said, 'In the name of Jesus Christ of Nazareth, give this man life.'

That evening, I opened my eyes for the first time in six days. I was confused and disorientated. My mam was by my bedside.

'What's going on? What am I doing here?'

'You won't believe what's happened to you!' she said.

She told me how ill I had been and about the Christians who had prayed for me.

'Who did they pray to?'

'God, or Jesus, I think,' she told me.

'Jesus? Why does Jesus want anything to do with a scumbag like me?' I thought if there was a God, He would only want to know the nice people who didn't swear, fight or steal.

'I don't know, son, but you can ask them yourself. They're coming back later.'

I drifted off to sleep, finally breathing by myself.

When Pete and Aiden returned, I asked them the same question.

'A healthy man doesn't need a doctor, but a sick man does,' said Aiden. 'Jesus came for the sinners and those that are really lost like you. Jesus loves them all. He loves you too and He was looking for you on that bench.'

What were these two on, acid or something? I tried to pull the sheets up so they didn't see me giggling. I thought they must have had more drink than I'd ever had!

I'd never had any belief in God. Despite my nana being very religious, it didn't have any influence on me. She used to talk to imaginary people anyway and Jesus, to me, was part of her illness – believing in something else that wasn't really there. I found it hard enough to believe in what I *could* see, let alone what I couldn't.

Anyway, there couldn't possibly be a God, because of all the unfair things that had happened to me. And what about my nana? She'd suffered illness for most of her life, dying at the age of fifty-six. If God was real and He was a God of love, why did He allow her to go through all this?

My nana once asked me to get confirmed as a Protestant, so I could have Holy Communion with her. I was expected to go through the ritual of it without any explanation of what it was all about. I was only a kid, but I tried, just to please her. I started the ten-week course, but ended up smoking with some lads behind the church instead.

Years later, I took my nana to Midnight Mass every Christmas – there were a lot of drunks around and I wanted to make sure she got home safely. I couldn't understand what she saw in it; there was a bloke at the front waving smoke around and walking up and down and they sung these really boring songs. I didn't have a clue what they were on about. Despite all that, my nana always came out looking really happy.

After she died, I lit a candle in church for her every Christmas and sat there crying. I didn't really link it to anything religious; it was out of respect for her. But I couldn't openly show my feelings so I had to do it in secret – someone came in the church once when I was there and I threatened to smash his face in. The only other time I went to church was to nick money from the collection. I also tried a few times to get money from the minister at the cathedral in the St Hilda's district. When that didn't work, I faked an injury; I put my arm in a false sling and went to visit him.

Later he told me that as I left, he looked out of the window and saw me swapping it to my other arm. I wasn't the only fake though. Soon after, he saw a lady who arrived in a wheelchair, stand up and climb the cathedral steps.

'I witnessed two miracles that day!' he said.

Religion was all the same to me, a pointless ritual. When I was in Durham Prison, some Buddhists came into my cell. I took the mick out of them and told them I liked their hairstyle – bald, like mine – but no way was I walking round in a sack and sandals. They had nothing to offer me.

But despite all my doubts, lying there in that hospital bed, I knew something was different. I felt different. Gradually, I began to realise what it was: I wanted to live! I'd come into hospital desperate to die and waiting for the drink to kill me, but now I actually wanted life. It was worth more than anything I'd ever had before – drink, drugs, possessions, money. It was quite a scary feeling; I didn't understand what was going on or what it was that I wanted to live for.

There was something else I knew for certain: I would never again drink, smoke or take drugs. I'd said that before, usually every night on the bench, but this time I was absolutely convinced. Something had changed. But what? Much later, thinking about the dreams I'd had while I was in a coma – the white room, the melting wax figure – I think God was releasing me from my past and giving me a new life. It would take a while for me to fully understand it, or accept it.

Pete and Aiden visited me every day. Aiden came on his bike and sat at the end of the bed, reading stories from the Bible to me. I enjoyed his company. They didn't force it;

they only talked about Jesus and the Bible in response to my questions. I didn't want to become a Christian, but I wanted my respect back. I knew I wouldn't drink again, but I thought I would get out of hospital, find a job and start enjoying my new life.

I kept asking them what they wanted from me when I got out. They said they didn't want anything. But I was curious: what was driving these two lads? They told me that lots of people were praying for me. I wanted to know why.

Sometimes, my street friends visited me. One brought me a bottle of White Lightning and I told him to take it away. Another brought me a joint; I didn't want that either.

'I want you to continue to smoke,' my consultant, Dr Cove Smith, advised me. 'I've heard reports that you're going to stop drinking, smoking and taking drugs, but if you try and stop all three, you might turn to one of them again and it might be the worst one. The next time you're brought in, you'll be in a box.'

I said, 'Look, doctor, I can't explain why, but I don't want to smoke either and I'm not going to.'

My recovery was slow at first. My whole body was numb from the neck down. My uncle John used to come and feed me and I had to wear a catheter. For the next seven weeks, I couldn't walk and had to lie on my back and be lifted by crane into the bath.

I asked my consultant every other day if I was going to die. I was really scared, especially when my whole body swelled up. The examining doctor produced a huge needle to take a sample from my stomach.

'This won't hurt a bit,' he reassured me.

Wrong! I gritted my teeth as he inserted the needle in what seemed to be agonising slow motion. I was given some new antibiotics and the swelling disappeared. Then something really freaky happened: my top layer of skin started peeling off. It was a mixture of dead skin and dirt – my whole palm came away one day. I was only 11.5 stone then. It was a far cry from when I was at my physical peak – 21.5 stone of solid muscle. I was now half the man I used to be, and even less without my top layer of skin and dirt.

The staff were amazed at my recovery. The nurses told me that I was basically dead in their eyes. They had never seen anything like it. I'd been critical and now here I was, laughing and joking with them. They told me about an alcoholic in the next room to me. He'd been brought in with alcohol poisoning, but was making a good recovery and walking around the hospital. Then one day, without warning, he had a relapse, slipped into a coma and died. Compared to me, he had hardly anything wrong with him.

'Have you seen the light now? Do you think God woke you up from that coma?' The staff knew I'd been prayed for.

'Nah, I don't want to be a Christian. I'm not bothered.' I just wanted to get out and get on with my life.

I had a body scan every week and my liver and kidneys were healing well. The muscles in my legs were very weak, so with the help of physiotherapy and my Zimmer frame, I managed a few steps each day. My eyesight was very blurred and I didn't realise at the time how bad my eyes really were. I ended up being registered as partially sighted.

Finally, after two months, I was well enough to leave. That was a relief. There were too many people dying in that place and I didn't want to be one of them. Everybody waved me goodbye and some of the nurses were crying. As I left in the ambulance, I felt a bit apprehensive. What if I had a relapse like that other alcoholic and died? However, the consultant had inspected the property I was going to be living in and arranged for someone to come every day to feed me and check me.

I rented part of my mate Brigsy's house in Eckert Avenue, Whinney Banks, over the road from the Ward family. When I saw it, I cried; they'd prepared it for me with a stereo, TV and video. I was so touched.

I was feeling better every day. I still used walking sticks and had to shuffle up and down the stairs on my bum because my legs were so weak. A physiotherapist was supposed to visit me regularly; he came once and had to climb over addicts smoking crack cocaine and injecting heroin to get to my room. I never saw him again. Later I kicked the drug addicts out. I didn't want them around any more.

Pete and Aiden visited me regularly and I was still curious about this Jesus fellow.

'How do you fancy Alpha?' Pete asked me one day. 'It's a course at our church that will help to answer a lot of your questions.'

Church? 'You've got to be joking!'

'You get a free meal every time you go.'

He knew how to persuade me! A free meal? I reckoned I could always eat and then go for a walk if I got bored.

*   *   *   *   *

'Where's the ———— toilet?'

The woman on the door stared in horror. A huge guy with tattoos and no front teeth was standing at the church entrance swearing at her. She nervously directed me inside.

We had a good laugh about this in later years – she told me that she was praying that the Lord would sort me out!

The Alpha course was at the Oakwood Centre in Eaglescliffe, run by Emmanuel Fellowship (now Tees Valley Community Church).

'What am I doing here?' I thought, as I sat down. I didn't

know anyone at the table and they were all chatting and being friendly. I felt out of place. Next to me was a guy with long hair and a black leather jacket. I looked at him suspiciously. As we ate our meal, he said, 'Is there any seconds?' I decided then that he must be a good lad. I later found out his name: Dave Benjamin. We became good friends.

I tried to sit at the end of the row when it was time for the talk. I wanted to make a quick getaway. But everyone else started coming in and asking me to move up, so I ended up being sat in the middle. I would feel a bit weird getting up and pushing past everyone to escape. I was stuck.

I listened to the talk, 'Why Did Jesus Die?' and suddenly realised I knew the leader, Martin Ruddock. He and his brother John lived where I used to knock about and they had been at my mate Smiggy's school.

I didn't say much that night. I realised I was the only one in the group who was swearing and it worried me.

'Sorry, I can't help it,' I said to the leaders.

'Don't worry, we're not offended by it,' I was told.

That was strange; I hadn't been bothered about offending anyone before.

I went back the next week and Martin invited a few of us to his house. He and his wife, Margaret, made me feel really at home. I could talk freely without being worried about my language. They accepted me as I was.

*   *   *   *   *

I was at the Wards' house – and I was worried.

'Lizzie, I think there's something wrong with me. I need to see a psychiatrist.'

'Why, what's up?' she said.

'I actually can't wait to get to that church tomorrow night and ask loads of questions.'

'Don't worry about it. It's because it's a new thing. It will wear off,' she reassured me.

Back at home, I glanced out of the window and spotted some kids running over the bridge to Teeside Retail Park behind the house. I used to shoplift there; I knew they were about to do the same. I suddenly had this really strange feeling in my heart. I wanted to rush over and tell them not to do it. What the flippin' heck was wrong with me?

I rushed back over the road.

'You won't believe this, Lizzie. Not only do I want to get back to this church, but I've just seen these kids going to nick stuff and I want to tell them not to do it any more.'

'Gram, don't worry,' she said. 'It's because you've been ill. It will pass.'

But I didn't want it to pass. It felt good – the sense of wanting to help someone in the right way, the way these people at church seemed to want to help me without asking anything from me.

I had to do something. I gathered all the estate kids together and told them that there was a better way to live other than shoplifting, drinking and taking drugs. They all laughed at me.

'What are you telling us for? You're the biggest culprit!' they said.

The truth was that I didn't really know why I was telling them. I just knew I had to.

By the fourth week of Alpha I started to feel that I really belonged to this group. I made more of an effort with my appearance; I bought myself some new clothes and my mate gave me some new trainers out of his shop. I had a shave, put on some aftershave; my hair was growing back, and I had my new false teeth!

*　　　*　　　*　　　*　　　*

It was a set-up; I was convinced of it. I'd been invited back to Mike Horner's house. He was one of the Christians who had taken me to hospital with my burnt leg. I'd asked to go to the toilet and in the bathroom were a gold watch, some rings and aftershave. They're watching me, waiting for me to nick it all, I thought. So I didn't.

'No one's going to catch me out!'

It wasn't until later that I realised they genuinely weren't bothered. They actually trusted me.

While I was at Mike's house, two ladies from Uganda were visiting. One of them was called Rose – she *rose* from the dead! She told me that in her village, sick people who couldn't be healed by the witch doctor were cast out. This happened to her and she died. Some Christians found her body, prayed for her and she came back to life.

Rose asked if they could pray for me. I stood up at first, but because my legs were so weak and shaky, I had to kneel down in the end. They prayed for ages in a strange language, also asking God to deliver me from evil spirits, and suddenly I started rising to my feet without even putting my hands on the floor – normally I couldn't stand without shuffling around and pulling myself up.

The fifth week of Alpha, Holy Spirit Day, was at Brockley Hall, Saltburn. I was apprehensive. What if all this wasn't real and didn't work? I had built my hopes up by this time. What if it's for everyone else and not for me?

I didn't want to feel disappointed and rejected.

'This is where the rubber hits the road now,' Martin told us that afternoon. 'If anyone wants to ask Jesus into their life, now is the time. Instead of just hearing about it, you can experience God for yourself and start a real relationship with Him.'

We were asked to stand up and hold out our hands. I desperately wanted it to be true, but I was scared in case nothing happened. All I'd heard up to this point was lots of words. I needed more than words.

I shut my eyes and said, 'Jesus, if you're real, words aren't enough. People have told me that they love me all my life, but I never really believed it. I really need to hear it from you that you love me. If you come into my life and show me that you love me, I promise that I'll tell everyone for the rest of my life on earth that you love them.'

'Go on, son, it's going to be OK.' It was my nana's voice! I had no idea where it had come from, but suddenly all my doubts disappeared and I felt so light that I fell back in my chair. There was something warm inside and suddenly it was all over me. The hairs on the back of my neck stood up, I had goose bumps and I suddenly started weeping. At first I had my hands over my face because I didn't want people to see me crying, but when I peered through the cracks in my fingers, I saw that other people were in tears, so I felt OK about it then.

I'd never wept so much in my life. I'd cried occasionally over the years, but a tough lad wasn't supposed to cry. When I was an alcoholic, I'd cry about anything – a leaf falling off a tree, a cat crossing the road – but the tears I shed now weren't tears of sadness or rejection, or the tears of a drunk: they were tears of joy, happiness and hope ... such an overwhelming sense of hope.

'Someone actually believes in me, someone's for me and loves me!'

It was everything I'd ever wanted and searched for my whole life. It was indescribable.

Before all this had happened, I'd asked Mike Horner what the time was. It was 2.45pm on 9 November 1996, the day my life was transformed. I was so happy and overwhelmed with love and joy. All my life I'd tried to reach this point and in the end it was so simple – I just asked Jesus into my life.

We shared Communion – my first ever. It was awesome, taking part in something that God had commanded us to do and acknowledging that Jesus' blood had washed me clean and His body was given for me. I couldn't keep this to myself.

*   *   *   *   *

'I'm a Christian! Jesus loves me and He loves you lot!'

I'd burst into the living room of the Wards' house. It was packed with people, who were all now staring at me.

'Gram, shut the ————— door will you,' said Lesley, turning back to the TV.

It wasn't long before the jokes started.

'The only reason you want to be a Christian is that there's plenty of parties in heaven!'

'You'll be wanting to change water into wine, knowing you.'

The teasing didn't bother me, but when Lesley swore, I felt a jolt inside and thought: what is she saying that for? It wasn't until later that night that I realised why it had made me feel uncomfortable; I'd stopped swearing. From swearing in every sentence and trying so hard for weeks to stop, it had gone completely. In fact, I lost 200 words of my vocabulary that night!

I was restless and desperate to get out. I rushed round to Pete Conroy's house. He opened the door and stared at me in amazement.

'Look at you!' He called his wife: 'Helen, come and look at Gram.'

'Why, what is it?' I asked, puzzled.

'You're full of Jesus!'

'Am I?'

'Yes!'

I was buzzing. I had to get to my bench. 'Pete, you've got to take me to the centre of Middlesbrough. I have to tell the drug addicts and prostitutes that Jesus loves them, because He's real.'

The night before, I'd met a couple of lads I'd known for years. One said, 'Hey Gram, I heard you're going to some kind of church, aren't you?'

'Nah, I'm just checking out this course.'

I was scared of talking about it, but now, twenty-four hours later, there was no stopping me. I started with the bench where I'd sat as an alcoholic for three and a half years and told the drug addicts gathered there that Jesus loved them. I went round the corner and told the bouncers on the door, pizza shop assistants and customers, police, passers-by, drinkers coming out of the pubs – I even stopped taxis to tell the drivers. For four hours I told everyone I could find. Pete, who'd come with me, was a bit stunned, but he was over the moon seeing what had happened to me.

Some old mates said: 'What you on about, Gram? Give your head a shake!' So instead of rumours that I was dead (which were still going round five years later) the word on the street was that I was brain damaged from the coma.

I couldn't sleep that night because I was so excited. I was desperate to get to church the next day, Sunday, and meet this family of God I'd been told about so much. It felt a bit strange at first. I didn't know the songs, there was a lot I didn't understand and I couldn't read the Bible, but it was still really exciting. Here was a room full of people who had the love of Jesus, just like me. It was so different from my experience of church in the past.

There was something that I'd struggled with on the Alpha course. I knew that I was a lost cause and needed Jesus, but what about the others? One man was a doctor earning good money, another woman had a nice job, home and kids, another bloke had a good job and a big Mercedes. They hadn't done anything wrong; why were they there? However, it became apparent that they all needed the same thing: Jesus. He had died for them too. They were just as lost without Him as I was, despite their appearance of success. We all became Christians on the same day and every one of us became a different person – the others were enjoying life more, had more peace, and didn't seem to worry about things in the same way. It wasn't just something that had happened to me.

I was out on the streets every day of the week after that, sometimes until 2am. I'd take the addicts hanging round the bench for coffee and talk to them about Jesus. Then Teen Challenge, a Christian group dedicated to working on the streets, asked me to help out. I joined them every Friday night on their bus, giving out soup, tea and coffee to my old friends. They would sometimes take me to one side and whisper: 'Gram, what are you up to? What are you getting out of this?'

'I'm not getting anything out of it. I know Jesus is real and I just want to help,' I told them.

They didn't believe me. 'Come on, Gram, we know you. What's going on?'

'First dead, then brain damaged and now I'm involved in a scam!' I said to myself.

I often got called Gram the Baptist or Abragram. I wasn't bothered; I'm sure I would have thought the same in their position. My desire to help them was greater than my desire to go back to being a drunk; they would realise the change was genuine when I didn't return to my old lifestyle. I had a powerful sense of challenge and mission from Jesus. I finally understood why I was born and why my life had been the way it was; it was so that I could use my experiences to help others and show them Jesus. I also understood what I'd felt for those lads running over the bridge that day: it was love. Jesus had given it to me and I wanted them to have what I had. It was what had motivated the Christians to keep talking to me and helping me when they saw me on my bench. God's love meant they wanted to give, not expecting anything in return.

Then Lesley Ward went to Low Newton Prison on remand. I told her mum, Lizzie, I would go and visit her, so I travelled to Durham on the bus six days a week, taking her clothes and other provisions. It gave me lots of opportunities to tell people on the bus about Jesus.

I wanted to learn more about Jesus by reading the Bible. However, because of my lack of effort at school, I couldn't read properly, and I was still partially sighted. Someone bought me a large-print Bible. The words were so big that the whole Bible was four books long. It became a bit of a joke at church.

'Gram, have you brought your Bible?'

'Yeah, which one?' I needed a wheelbarrow for them all!

Patrick Hinton, who'd set up Teen Challenge locally, bought me Luke's Gospel on tape and I listened to it every night. I looked at the words as I heard them and gradually taught myself to read from God's Word. Patrick also bought me the large-print version of Selwyn Hughes' *Every Day with Jesus* [1] which had some Bible verses and teaching for every day of the year. I read this every morning and then read the same portion again at night. I learned that the Bible was like spiritual food and I was hungry for more. My only other use for the Bible in the past was to smoke it when I was in solitary, but now I understood its power for the first time. It fed me and the words were changing me; gradually I was growing as a Christian and growing to know and love Jesus more. I'd sometimes lie in the dark and talk to Jesus for hours. I got up early and spent several hours in the morning and again at night, praying and learning to read.

My new Christian friends helped me a great deal. Martin Ruddock started teaching me and I travelled round with him while he preached; he's a very gifted communicator. I also started giving talks about what had happened to me.

Patrick Hinton was fantastic. He owned a chain of fifty supermarkets – Hinton's – but was very down-to-earth and friendly; I called him Mr Hinton, but he insisted that I call him Patrick. He became like a spiritual father to me and taught me so much. Once, after I shared my story with some addicts, he said to me: 'Gram, there will come a time when you can speak using Bible verses and remember where they are.' I thought there'd be no chance of that. But he was right. He also encouraged me to stay humble. He said: 'Your name's going to go all over. But keep everything in your heart, not your head. If it's in your head, it'll be all about you; if it's in your heart, it'll be all about Jesus.'

We were barred from a shop once. I was refused a refund for a T-shirt, because it had been bought more than fourteen days ago. I wasn't happy.

'You think I'm scum, don't you?' I told the shop assistant. 'How about I burn your shop down?'

'Go over there and be quiet, Gram,' said Patrick. He calmly turned to the manager. 'I think you'd better fax me your rules and regulations. You can't see them because they are hidden by these boxes.'

We were given a refund, and told never to come back. Patrick taught me that you can get results in the right way without kicking up a fuss. He died on 3 August 2004, aged seventy-seven. He was a wonderful man and still very much missed. His wife, Jane, is still very supportive of my work with her wisdom and love. She was, and still is, like a spiritual mother to me.

*   *   *   *   *

One day, I was sitting on my bench with Aiden, talking about the baptism of the Holy Spirit and the gift of tongues, and what it all meant, when suddenly I said something in a language I'd never used before.

I remembered the first time I'd heard it: 'Rose from the dead', the Ugandan lady, had prayed for me using a strange language.

'Why didn't those ladies pray in English?' I had asked Pete Conroy on the way home.

'Er, I don't know, mate,' he'd muttered as he drove. As I wasn't a Christian at the time, I don't think I would have understood what 'speaking in tongues' was all about.

After those first few words spoken on my bench, I prayed again when I was alone on my bed. I started making strange noises, like a baby. It was a language I didn't recognise. My understanding of tongues – speaking in a language you have never learned – is that it's an intimate way for us to communicate with the Lord, without anyone else (or even ourselves) knowing what we are saying. It's a privilege to be able to use this; it's one of the supernatural gifts given by a loving God to change our lives.[2]

I've not only seen God's miraculous power in my own life, but also in the lives of many others. Once I was helping a family where the children had drug problems. The grandmother, Nana Jean, was sixty-one and a Catholic – she belonged to a church and believed that God existed, but didn't have a personal relationship with Him. I got to know her and she made a commitment to the Lord. She had terrible arthritis in her skull and really bad headaches.

One day, I prayed very simply for her to be healed. She never had another headache after that. She came away with us to an Alpha course – I was helping out on them by now. She was bad on her feet and had a stair-lift in her house, but she came back from the Holy Spirit Day and ran up and down the stairs! She was completely healed.

*   *   *   *   *

That December, my uncles called me to a meeting. They had all phoned my mam to ask what was wrong with me. They noticed that I had a peace about me and I was different. I was able to tell them why. My mam knew I'd become a Christian. She couldn't quite believe it at first. She said to Patrick Hinton, 'I keep thinking I'm dreaming.'

Patrick said, 'Well, pinch yourself, Pat, because you're not dreaming. It's Jesus.'

A lot of my family and friends thought that if it helped me personally to live a better life, then great. They didn't really understand that they could have the relationship with God that I now had. I'd said sorry to both my mam and my step-dad, Dave, for everything I'd done to them in the past. My relationship with Dave had really improved, especially when I was in hospital. There was a little black and white portable in my room and he bought a brand-new colour TV for me. That meant such a lot. I finally realised that Dave Lawson wanted the same thing for my mam that I did – for her to be happy – yet all those years I was convinced that he was taking her away from me.

Christmas 1996 was absolutely awesome. The previous year, I'd been crawling on my hands and knees desperate to find a drink. This year, I was completely free. I finally understood the meaning of Christmas; it wasn't about the material things that I thought I'd lost when I was a tramp.

It was about the birth of Jesus and what He'd done for us all. And I wasn't alone any more; I had this massive new family of God.

I knew I had so much to do. That Christmas morning I fed the homeless at church. My heart was bleeding when I saw them go back to drinking and wandering the streets. I knew how that felt and it made me more determined to try and help them. I'd cried out to God and become more burdened for them and more determined to help them. I knew I had to meet them where they were at ... where I used to be.

As I retraced my steps, I found myself back in court, the place where I'd stood defiantly in front of so many magistrates, lied through my teeth and acted as if I didn't care what happened.

This time, though, I had something very different to say.

1. *Every Day with Jesus* – bimonthly Bible devotional notes written by Selwyn Hughes are still published by CWR. See www.cwr.org.uk

2. The baptism in the Holy Spirit, with the associated manifestation of spiritual gifts such as speaking in languages previously unknown and unlearned, is an experience Jesus promised to His followers. The baptism is given for powerful and effective ministry. See Acts 1:8; 2:1–21; 1 Corinthians 12,14.

CHAPTER NINE

BACKYARD MISSION

You wouldn't have thought of putting us together. I'm 5ft4 and from Essex, he's 6ft5 and from Middlesbrough. But the Lord knew what he was doing. My dad told me once: 'I don't believe in all this Christian stuff, but since you met Gram, you've got everything you ever wanted.' It's an awesome ministry and I'm so glad to be part of it. It's absolutely amazing thinking about where we've come from to where we are now.'

Natasha Seed

I knew they were 'boys' as soon as I saw them – Lacoste jumpers, Burberry jackets – I recognised the dress code. Hardened criminals, silently glaring at me as I approached them.

I'd joined Martin Ruddock at the Salt and Light Bible College in Haddington, East Lothian, where he taught on evangelism (telling people about Jesus). Out on the streets with the students, I turned to Martin: 'Door knocking isn't really my cup of tea. Do you mind if I go to the local courts?'

'That's fine, Gram. I know it's where you want to be.'

When I arrived, I found the toilets, shut the door and did something that I still do to this day. I got on my knees and said, 'Lord Jesus, can You help me talk to someone in here about You? I can't do it by myself.'

I soon spotted a group of about nine lads hanging about. I walked over. 'Now lads, you can probably tell from my accent that I'm from Middlesbrough.' They glared at me and said nothing. I continued. 'I'm a born-again Christian and I'm just telling people about Jesus and I want to pray that you lads get justice today and that there's no corruption. I've been in jail and ...'

One of them stopped me and said, 'Have you been in Durham jail?'

'Yeah, loads of times.'

'Were you there in 1988?'

I told him I was. He said, 'I used to train in the gym with you. You were massive! What's your name again?'

'Gram.'

'That's it, Big Gram! Lads, it's Big Gram!' He was smiling and shaking my hand – so were the others. I stood and prayed for all nine of them in the middle of the court buildings. I didn't want to leave them, but I had to get back to the others. Later, when we were on the streets, one of the lads approached me.

'Our Gram, thanks for praying,' he said. 'You know I told you I was at court for nicking cars and it wasn't me? I had nicked a car ages ago, but not this one. I was going to go to jail today, but they threw it out of court.'

Later, I saw one of the others.

'Gram, your prayers, man, they worked,' he said. 'You know I was meant to have bottled someone in a pub and I wasn't there?'

'Yeah, I've heard that one before,' I said.

'Honestly,' he said. 'I'd tell you, Gram, if I did. I was with my girlfriend but they wouldn't use her statement. I went before the sheriff today and I was going to get twelve months and he said he'd heard that there was another statement and why hadn't it been read out. He insisted on seeing it and asked if there were any witnesses to the incident. The defence had a statement from the landlord and a description of the lad. The sheriff said: "What have you been doing? You're just wasting my time today. Case dismissed." I can't believe it, Gram!'

'That's Jesus. He loves you and don't you ever forget it.'

*   *   *   *   *

I believe I met an angel in Haddington. My friend Lizzie Ward's two-year-old granddaughter, Renee, had a terrible accident. Lizzie was looking after her and turned her back for a few minutes. Renee had crawled up the stairs, climbed up on the bunk beds and fallen out of a window. She was rushed to hospital with a fractured skull and was in a coma.

Lizzie wouldn't go to the hospital because she felt so guilty about what had happened. I decided to send her a card. I went to the post office and behind the counter there was a man and a small, plump woman with dark curly hair. I told her I needed a postcode and she pulled out a postcode book straight away.

It's a funny sounding name – Eckert Avenue,' I said.

'Here it is,' she said, almost immediately without asking the spelling.

'Are you sure it's the right spelling, because it's very unusual?'

'That's the one,' she reassured me.

I sent the card to Lizzie, who then visited her granddaughter in hospital. She woke up and eventually recovered.

A couple of days later I went to the post office again; only the man was there. I told him I wanted to say thanks for the postcode.

'That's funny,' he said. 'We don't have any postcodes for England, only this area and Edinburgh.'

I started feeling angry, thinking he was calling me a liar.

'I'm telling you there was a woman in here the other day who gave me the postcode.'

I described her and he said: 'There's only one woman working here and she's tall and blonde.' Everyone else was saying: 'Are you sure it's the right post office, Gram?'

'Yeah, it's right by the outreach. We've been outside here every day.'

The guy from the post office said, 'Listen, it was either a robber or a ghost … and we haven't been robbed.'

I believe that angels are part of the divinity of God. They are not white, fluffy creatures with wings; they could look like any of us. The book of Hebrews in the Bible, chapter 13, tells us to be careful who you speak to, because you could be entertaining angels. I remember one story I heard was about a lady who used to go round the roughest parts of the Bronx telling people about Jesus. One day, someone approached her and said, 'I'm a Christian now. Where's the two black guys that were with you when you used to prayer walk round the streets?' She said that she never travelled round with any black guys; she worked on her own. She believed they were angels.

The second time I had an encounter with an angel was after I'd had a tooth pulled and I thought I was getting septicaemia again. I had a lump in my throat and my mouth swelled up. I prayed for ages that I would get healed. I was in bed that night and I felt someone pushing me against the wall. I woke up and could hear: 'Shhhh, Gram's not well; he's laid in bed bad.' The next day I was completely healed.

I found a new home that year. The council didn't want to give me a flat because of my past behaviour, but one member of staff, Claire James, heard my story and worked really hard to get one for me. In fact, she got me a double flat because she knew I was a big lad. I was claiming incapacity benefit and managing to survive on £20 a week for food.

I even managed to save up and bought clothes at the end of the month. I wasn't bothered about money. My heart was so moved and desperate to help people that if I got a normal job, I wouldn't have enough time to talk to people on the streets, as I did every day. I always took eight booklets out each day called *Why Jesus?* and wouldn't go home unless eight people had taken them and said the sinner's prayer at the back.

My baptism on 29 June was fantastic. Friends and family were there, including my mam, who had retired and moved to Portugal by then. As I stood at the front, she was crying and saying to people around her: 'That's my son!' After everything I'd done to hurt and disappoint her in the past, I'd finally made my mother proud. I'd never done it before and it really moved me.

Two other friends who came to my baptism were Tony and Hayley – they had tried to help me after Tony had found me on the streets as a tramp. I never rammed the Bible down their throats, but simply by being the new Gram, my actions spoke louder than my words. Tony and Hayley became Christians a week after my baptism and married at our church. They'd seen me struggle all my life and wanted what Jesus had given me.

At the end of 1997 I felt I needed to learn more; I'd been out on the streets every day for a year now, but I needed more knowledge. Patrick had also asked me to work for Teen Challenge, but wanted me to have some training first. I found out about a three-month college course, after which students spent some time working abroad. I thought it sounded brilliant. It started in April and I knew that God would provide money to pay for it if He wanted me to go. Without me knowing, Patrick had already decided to pay for it.

*   *   *   *   *

'Your mission is in your back yard.'

I was in the court gallery on Boxing Day when the words came into my head. I was thinking about what they meant, when suddenly I heard: 'All you've done for the last few years is take drugs, steal, drink and cause a nuisance on the streets of Middlesbrough and today we're going to have to remand you in custody.' I looked down at the lad stood in front of the magistrate. I knew then God had used this situation to speak to me: I wasn't to go on this college course. God wanted me to stay in Middlesbrough, where these people needed help.

I carried on with the street work and travelling with Martin. Sometimes we visited gospel businessmen's lunches and schools and I was telling my story more regularly. The new word round town was that I needed some good alibis – I was going to do some big job and bring a load of drugs in. It brought it home to me how real the change in my life was. If I was exactly the same, they wouldn't be talking about me.

I'd heard about the Teen Challenge School of Evangelism, which ran a ten-week course in Essex but I didn't think anything more about it or even pray about it – I believed that God had told me to stay in Middlesbrough. I was a young Christian and had misunderstood what God had said: He didn't want me to go on the previous course, but it didn't mean I wasn't to go on *this* one. But God was going to make sure I got the message. My friend, David Dodsworth, approached me one day and said: 'I believe God wants to tell you to just go.' I wasn't sure at the time what to make of that.

One morning as I was praying and reading my Bible, the message in *Every Day with Jesus* was about Mary visiting the empty tomb. There was an angel there, who said to go and tell the disciples that Jesus was waiting for them in Galilee. Later, as I waited for the bus, it struck me: 'Jesus is waiting for me in Essex!' I remembered what David Dodsworth had said: 'Just go.' I went straight home and phoned Patrick. I was about to spend the longest time I'd ever spent in a classroom – and meet the wonderful woman who was about to become part of my life.

*   *   *   *   *

I was off to Essex and I'd just spotted the biggest burglar in Whinney Banks. Who better to look after my flat?

'Carl, I'm going to London for a few weeks. Would you keep an eye on my flat?'

'Yeah, course I will, Gram.'

Pete and Helen Conroy, who had picked me up, were stunned. 'Why are you telling him?'

'He's the best one to know. I've grown up with him and I know he's going to watch out for me,' I told them.

That September in Essex was absolutely brilliant. Sitting in the Teen Challenge School of Evangelism, I not only learned so much more about Jesus, who I loved more than anyone, but also how to communicate better with people on the streets. I shared a room with a great lad called Lee, a recovering alcoholic who now works at a rehab and charity called Betel. We used to give our testimonies at local churches to raise sponsorship.

On one visit, I was told about an alcoholic, currently in a coma at King George Hospital, Ilford. Would I visit him if he woke up? He was called Jason Pratley. He was found unconscious in a garage; he'd been drinking methylated spirits and his insides had shut down. He'd been in prison for murder and his wife and kids had left him. He later told me that he used to go and sit by the River Thames, fishing, and often contemplated jumping in. I knew exactly how he felt.

'Can I have a fag?' Jason looked at me and repeated his request for the next fifteen minutes. He had a beard and tattoos all over his face. I tried to talk to him, but he wasn't really listening. I decided to show him the photos of me when I was in a coma. I turned to get them and as I turned back to look at him, I nearly fainted. Suddenly it wasn't Jason in the hospital bed. It was me. I started weeping and praying, 'Jesus, help me to help him.'

I felt God tell me to read Acts 3 to him, so I got a Bible from the nurse. I read to him about the beggar by the Gate called Beautiful where the apostle Peter said in verse 6: 'Silver or gold I do not have, but what I have I give to you. In the name of Jesus Christ of Nazareth, walk.'

'I'm telling you Jason, I haven't got nowt for you,' I told him. 'I can't give you a fag, but what I have got is Jesus and I really want you to know Him. Do you want to pray?'

He agreed, held out his hands and gave his life to Jesus. He was weeping and his face started changing, becoming more relaxed and peaceful. He told me he felt so much happier and asked me to come the next day and read the Bible to him.

I cleared it with the nurse first.

'You can take him for a fag if you like,' she said.

'No, don't tell him that!' I said.

I went back again and asked if he was sure he wanted me to come back. He said, 'Definitely! I want to know more about Jesus.'

The next night, he wasn't in the room. The sister came to see me and said, 'I've got some bad news. We went in an hour after you left to give him a drink and he'd died.'

'That's good,' I told her. 'At least he's gone to heaven.'

'What do you mean?'

For the next half hour I told her and the other nurses about Jesus and having a sure hope of going to heaven. I felt sad that he'd died, but I felt God saying to me, 'Don't worry, he's with Me now, but I want you to continue doing what you did with those nurses.'

Three weeks before the end of the course, I visited Ilford Elim City Gates Church. The pastor, Steve Derbyshire, said, 'Right, church, go and find someone you've never spoken to before and say good morning.'

'Hi, my name's Natasha,' said a blurred woman; I couldn't see her properly.

I said, 'Hi, I'm Gram, from Middlesbrough. Listen, if I don't say hello to you any more, it's not that I'm ignoring you. I just can't see you properly. If you see me next week, come and say hello and I'll tell you my story.'

For the past two years I'd been registered as partially sighted with Middlesbrough Social Services – the retina nerves at the back of my eyes had decayed when I was in the coma. I sat really close to the TV so that I could see it and I had a talking watch and a talking alarm clock with an annoying American voice that did my head in.

It was nearly time to go home. I lay in the dark on my own in the social room/chapel of the evangelism school and prayed: 'Lord, I'm really glad I came here. I've learned so much. Do You know what, Lord? I'm not really bothered about my eyesight. I've been praying to get it back every day since I came out of hospital. It would be like the icing on the cake to have my eyesight back. But it's not up to me, it's up to You. Just help me to be a good disciple of Yours and a good witness.'

The other students arrived and switched on the light. I couldn't believe it. I shut my eyes and covered my face with my hands. I didn't dare open them in case it wasn't real.

They all crowded round me. 'What's wrong, Gram?'

'I'm scared. When you put the light on I could see.'

'Go on, Gram, just look.' They all put their hands on me and started praying. I opened my eyes. 'Yes, I can see!' My eyesight was completely normal. God had healed me!

Middlesbrough Social Services didn't believe me. I've still got my partially sighted certificate to prove it.

*   *   *   *   *

Graduation was fantastic. It was at the City Gates Church and some of my friends travelled 250 miles for the occasion. I was told that someone was looking for me: Natasha, her sister Naomi and Naomi's boyfriend, Ike. I chatted to them and left to meet some friends at Burger King. As I turned to go, I really felt God say to me: 'Give them your phone number.' I wrote it down and handed it over. I said, 'I don't know why I'm giving you this, but if you're ever in Middlesbrough give us a ring and I'll meet you and have a coffee with you.'

Natasha called the next day to see if I'd got home all right but I wasn't in. She left a message. I rang her back, but *she* wasn't in, this time. She called me again and we chatted for three hours – the time just flew by. We phoned each other every night after that for the next month. I began to feel that this was something really special, and I still didn't even know what she looked like! She'd been blurred the first time and the second time I met her, it was dark in that part of the church and there were also so many people, I'd forgotten what I'd seen of her. I even had the cheek to ask her to send me a photograph.

She told me a few weeks later what had happened. As soon as I came in the church, God said: 'That's your husband.' She had only seen me from the back. She said to God, 'I'm not going to give him my address and phone number. If this is from you, I want him to give me his.'

She'd told her sister what God had said.

'You've got some faith!' she said.

That December she came to Middlesbrough. Tony took me to meet her at the train station. He expected me to be really nervous. I was shy with girls; it had been the drink that gave me confidence in the past. He couldn't believe it. As soon as she got off the train, I was slapping her lips.

It didn't feel awkward or strange; it felt like my girlfriend had been away and was coming home. It also turned out that everything I prayed to have in a wife, God had already told her. She knew I had a calling on my life to set the captives free and that she'd have to move to the area and support me in my ministry.

She then had the pleasure of meeting my old mates! Katy, a lesbian prostitute, looked her up and down and said, 'Who's this, Gram? She's a bit of all right.'

'This is my girlfriend, Natasha,' I told her.

We walked round the corner and bumped into this big hard lad I'd known for years.

'What team does she support then, Gram?' he growled.

'I don't like football,' Natasha said.

'She'll be supporting the Boro'!' I told him.

'Just as well!'

I really fell in love with her on that visit. I knew for certain that she was 'the one'. It was wonderfully romantic, almost like a childhood relationship. We'd agreed as Christians that we weren't going to have sex before marriage. This was something new. In the past, I'd get girls into bed as quickly as possible, but this time we were building proper foundations, a strong platform of love. We agreed that God had created sex for marriage and it would be a bonus to what we'd already built up. I'd tried to explain this to Katy when we met her, but she couldn't believe we weren't sleeping together.

'Gram, come on, we know you.'

'Katy, what you know is the old Gram, not the new one. I'm a Christian now and I'm trying to do what the Bible says.'

I knew I was a new creation in God. Natasha had never slept with anyone and I'd never slept with anyone as a Christian, so in the Lord's eyes we were virgins and pure before Him. I believe that it made it really special for us. Your wife is someone to love, honour and respect, whereas I didn't have any respect for any of the women I'd been involved with previously.

On 8 January 1999 – Natasha's birthday – I was sitting in her Essex flat wearing a vest and a pair of shorts, scoffing a Chinese takeaway. I was about to propose!

'You know you said you'd follow me and support me if we got married?' I mumbled at her, chow mein falling out of my mouth. 'Will you marry me, then?'

I wasn't much good at the romantic stuff. And I'd never learned any table manners. In fact, I'd hardly ever eaten at a table. Growing up and in various prison cells, I ate alone, so I was used to chomping it down and not talking to anyone. Once, Patrick Hinton invited me round to talk to this hard lad and out of twenty-two bags of crisps, I ate twenty-one of them. We had steak and chips after that and I got a piece of steak stuck in my throat. I pulled it out and my false teeth came with it.

'That's it. I've never seen anything like him!' said this lad, who'd been watching me. It gave me an opening to tell him my story and he became a Christian that night.

But my table manners didn't always have such a positive result – especially when I met my future in-laws for the first time.

'He doesn't eat like us, does he?' said Natasha's mum, watching me; they were all eating properly and chatting over their meal. I wasn't.

After the meal, Natasha's mum said, 'Right Gram, what did you used to do, then?'

Natasha said straight out in her lovely southern accent, 'You used to be a hooligan, didn't you, darling?'

'Yeah, I went to university to study it.'

We all laughed and for the next two hours I told them all about my life. They sat there with their mouths open. They had the same expression two days later. I'd just asked them if I could marry their daughter. They spent the next hour trying to talk us out of it.

Suddenly, God prompted me to speak. I told them, 'Listen, I really love your daughter. I'd never hurt her and I want to do the best for her. I promise you if she was ever depressed and couldn't handle it and she wanted to come back, I'd pack up whatever I was doing and bring her straight back to you. I'll make sure she visits you at least eight times a year; I'll make provision for that.'

They gave us their blessing then and celebrated with champagne. I drank orange.

I went home to prepare for the wedding. Some nights I was too excited to sleep, thinking about my love for Natasha and dreaming about our future life together. It gave me a greater love for God and a stronger determination to tell people about Jesus' love.

*   *   *   *   *

'I hope she's not late. I might think she's changed her mind!'

It was 19 June 1999. I was standing at the front of our church, nervously waiting for my bride. As she came down the aisle, I couldn't resist it, I had to look. I turned round and saw such an amazing picture of beauty coming towards me. As she lifted up her veil, I felt so blessed that this beautiful woman loved me and wanted to marry me. Our vows were so special. It was what I'd wanted all my life – knowing someone was there for me. Next to saying 'I will' to the Lord and following Him, Natasha saying 'I will' to me and becoming my bride was the best thing that had ever happened to me.

About 700 family, friends and church family were with us. It was brilliant – apart from the fight.

'Don't nick at our Gram's wedding!' a lass shouted at a girl trying to nick a handbag. It could only happen at my wedding!

We had our honeymoon in Portugal and returned to live in my flat in Whinney Banks.

I was still helping out on the Teen Challenge bus every week. One night Natasha rang me. 'Gram, there's someone in our front room.'

The next minute I heard a male voice on the line.

'Hi Gram, I'm just checking on things like you asked me to.' It was Lee, the mate I'd asked to keep an eye on the flat and Natasha while I wasn't there.

'Thanks mate, but can you knock on the door next time. She's not like us.'

Natasha had most of the madmen in Whinney Banks looking out for her. But getting used to the area and being faced with the consequences of my past was a bit of a culture shock. We were followed by police and security when we went into town and I often heard my name mentioned over the two-way radios. Natasha sometimes thought I was being paranoid. But one day in the Next store, she saw the evidence for herself. I was being followed again.

'Natasha, this guy following us is going to come through that clothes rack in a minute.' She didn't believe me. Suddenly, 'as if by magic' he appeared through the clothes – just like the shopkeeper in the children's TV show, *Mr Ben*.

'I don't steal any more, mate,' I told him.

This carried on for years, even when we had children. Natasha was followed all round town once when she was pushing a pram. Another time, I was putting some shoes on my son's feet in a shop and suddenly it came over the security guards' radio: 'Gram Seed's bending over. What's he doing?' Security staff came over to stare at me. 'I'm just trying some shoes on my son,' I told them.

We wanted children straight away, but I wasn't sure I could have them. I'd tried to get girls pregnant in the past because I thought it was a way to get love. I remember once in jail a little kid ran up to a prisoner, put his arms round him, and said, 'Daddy, Daddy, I love you.' I wanted someone to do that to me. But it didn't happen.

However, Natasha fell pregnant immediately, and I realised God had been watching over the situation all these years, even before I knew Him. We were delighted, although I was worried about her; she had a difficult pregnancy. I also worried about being a good dad. Suppose my dad not being around had affected me and I couldn't love my child?

On 5 May 2000, our son Caleb was born. Natasha had to have a Caesarean. He was massive – 11lb2 and 2ft long. The consultant said, 'This isn't a baby, it's a toddler!' Then Caleb weed on him.

As soon as I held Caleb in my arms, I loved him. But more than that – suddenly, for the first time, I really experienced and understood the father's love that God had for me. I'd never been able to relate to that before because of my past. But that day, a new process of healing began. But I knew that if God was to heal me completely there was something else I had to do; something that had been hanging over me for more than thirty years.

*   *   *   *   *

'Good riddance to him,' I'd said, angrily. I'd just learned that my dad had died.

I had no intention of going to his funeral, but my mother-in-law, Barbara, gave me some really good advice. She said, 'If you don't go, and you regret it, you can never go again. But if you *do* go and you regret it, you can just get over it.'

I knew she was right. And there was something important I needed to go for. However, arriving at the church I felt so awkward that I hid in the bushes. When everyone had gone inside, I slipped in unnoticed and sat in one of the back pews. I was ready – I knew what I had to do. Before God, I finally forgave my father for hurting my mam and abandoning me. I also repented of all the negative thoughts and feelings I'd had towards him since I was a child.

I wanted to leave before anyone saw me, but suddenly the service finished and everyone turned to go. They all stopped and stared at me as if they had seen a ghost. I hurried out, but two ushers came running after me and said my dad's sister, Margaret, wanted to talk to me.

I think they were all a bit wary of me, but I reassured them that I was a Christian and needed to come and forgive my dad. Margaret was really touched. 'It sounds strange,' she said tearfully. 'But my brother was an alcoholic and died a horrible, lonely death in his flat, suffering from cancer. But it's really made my day seeing you here.'

The next day, I felt so different. I felt lighter and freer and my work had more of God's power in it. I'd learned how powerful forgiveness is in setting us free. The spiritual hold that was on me from my dad had gone. I hadn't even known it was there.

Our second son, Boaz, was born on 22 October 2003, weighing 9lb.

'Is that all he weighs?' I said.

The nurse looked at me strangely.

'That's big, Mr Seed.'

Not compared to our first he wasn't.

The Caesarean didn't go well; they couldn't seem to stop the bleeding. But God was already comforting Natasha. The anaesthetist had told her she was a Christian, after spotting me reading the Bible. Natasha knew God was with her.

However, I was sitting outside, worried sick. 'What if it all goes wrong? What if I lose her?'

I prayed for help. Suddenly the lift doors nearby opened. No one was there, but immediately I felt the most wonderful, warm feeling all over me – a real sense of the love and the presence of God. Why He came up in a lift, I don't know! But I knew then that my wife and new son were completely in God's hands; they were safe. I wasn't afraid any more. Everything was going to be all right.

CHAPTER TEN

'LET ME IN!'

'Gram was one of the firstfruits of the whole area and I think God plucked him out of his situation and chose him to take that message to others.'
Pete Conroy, evangelist

'You're going back to prison.'

'Oh no!' I never expected to hear that again. What could they possibly get me for this time?

I'd been standing at the front of our church. I always wanted more of God. Any call for prayer and I'd be out there – headaches, backaches, pre-menstrual tension – I'd take prayer for anything!

Jean had been a visitor to our church back in 1997. She was so small that she had to stand on the steps to pray for me. God had given her a message.

'Don't worry,' she'd reassured me. 'You're not going back as a prisoner. You're going to set the captives free.'

It was just what I wanted to hear. I was desperate to get back inside; I wanted to tell the lads about Jesus. However, I knew with my record it would be impossible without God; all I was able to do was see friends in the visitors' centres. But when Jean gave me that message, I knew it was from God. Jean didn't know anything about me or my background.

The following year, it happened; the miracle I'd been praying for.

My story had shocked the town; one minute I was an

alcoholic tramp, football hooligan and general nutter, and the next I was a non-drinking, non-smoking Christian, helping people on the streets and going into local schools. (I've had quite a bit of involvement with schools over the years; I teach six classes on the subject 'Is God real?' at Acklam Grange School, Middlesbrough each year and often help with drugs awareness courses at St Michael's School, Wolviston. Most other schools, however, don't ask me back a second time because I'm only allowed to mention Jesus once. He's mentioned at least twenty times in my story!)

It wasn't long before all this reached the local newspaper, *The Evening Gazette*; there was a picture of me sitting on my bench, grinning, under the headline 'Saving Grace'. While I was at the evangelism school, the article found its way to Les Frost, the governor at Holme House. A couple of months later, when I was back in Middlesbrough, he invited me into the prison to give a talk in the chapel.

Walking past the house blocks where I'd been locked up a few years previously, it all came rushing back; the banging of the cell doors, the sound of keys turning in the locks, the unbearable sense of being confined and restricted. It was horribly intimidating. Since that first visit, back in November 1998, I've felt the same oppression every time I enter the prison; I think God's allowed it so I can have more compassion and understanding of what the lads are going through.

The first time I spoke in the chapel, the lads were so gobsmacked that they sat there for an hour and never moved or said a word. Governor Frost came to listen; he said he'd never seen anything like it.

'I wish I could do another sentence,' I said, on the way out. I didn't want to leave those lads. That week, the chaplain rang me, on request from the governor, and asked if I wanted to come in every Thursday. I was over the moon.

Then more doors started opening. I was sharing my story at our church one day, when Lynne Brown approached me. She was one of the head social workers at a prison called Hassockfield Secure Training Centre, for twelve- to sixteen-year-olds. Was I interested in coming in? I didn't need asking twice!

Travelling to Hassockfield, in Consett, for the first time, I managed to get lost. Eventually, I got back on track, but as I came over the brow of the hill, it all seemed strangely familiar. Had I been here before? I didn't recognise the building. I gave my name at the gate and asked the security guard if anything else had ever been on this site.

'Medomsley Detention Centre,' he told me.

I nearly fell over! I was stunned. The Lord had brought me back to the place where it had all begun nearly twenty years before. But this time I was here to help. 'God, you're awesome,' I said and started laughing.

The guard was looking at me strangely. 'That's Jesus for you, mate,' I told him. He looked at me even more strangely then. He must have warned them inside that there was a nutcase waiting to come in.

I met the director, John Wade, and the other social workers. I started going in twice a month at first and eventually was invited in every week. Now I meet all the new lads and tell them who I am and how I can help. I get referrals from social workers when lads have asked to see me, give talks and run Bible studies. I also help the psychologist in afternoon group sessions, tackling subjects like bullying, addiction and disability awareness. I bring examples of mates that have died from drug overdoses, or girls I know on the streets, but I always bring the Christian message of hope and show them that there's a better way to live.

But there are restrictions when you are talking to children

about Jesus; the staff have to monitor what visitors are telling them, understandably. Each lad has such a lot of support – social workers, the Youth Offending Team, psychologists – you could get up to nine people behind each little prisoner, so it's been very much a case of us all working as a team. But God has given me some brilliant ideas to reach the kids. Once He gave me a Christian play that just dropped into my head one day. We've performed it a couple of times and it's gone down really well. Every year I organise something called Party in the Hack, a bit like Party in the Park. We have a barbecue, Christian bands, rap singers and an It's a Knockout competition. We also have a game called 'Which Life would You Choose?' which is based on my life before and after I became a Christian. If they want to know more about Jesus, they can write their name on a piece of paper and put it in a box for me to follow them up afterwards. I get about twenty responses each time.

One morning, about 6.30am, the phone rang. It was Norman, the deputy director. 'Gram, we need you to come over now.' They had found a fourteen-year-old lad hanging in his cell. As soon as I arrived, I was taken to the sports hall. It was full of children and staff. I was asked to do a service. I was totally unprepared. I didn't even have my Bible with me. I asked to go to the toilet and in the cubicle I got on my knees and said, 'Lord, what can I do? What can I say?'

'Gram, just open your mouth and I'll fill it,' He told me.

When I stood in front of everyone, I spoke about the value of unity and love in this desperate situation. Everyone was feeling the same way and it seemed to really touch them.

This was the youngest death ever in custody and, after a long investigation (which concluded in 2007), a number of changes were made nationally to the way juveniles are dealt with. But after this tragedy I realised that I was viewed as someone who acted like a Christian minister, rather than another helper or social worker. That meant a lot to me. It showed me that Jesus was making a difference and I was taken seriously for my faith. In fact, for five years, I was the next best thing they had to a chaplain. They've got one now, Stuart Bennett, who is a great bloke and we work really well together. In April 2007 I was officially taken on as a member of staff one day a week and they have now given me my own keys, which is amazing for an ex-con.

I really feel for those kids. I hear some tragic stories about how they've been physically and sexually abused, been in children's homes and faced life on the streets. It makes mine look like a choirboy's upbringing. To see their damaged little lives really cuts me up, especially having children of my own. I always wish I could do more, but I remind myself not to keep wishing, but to keep praying; I have to talk to God about people, before I talk to people about God.

My involvement in other prisons came through word of mouth. The chaplaincy at Holme House was asked to cover Kirklevington Grange, a resettlement jail for over twenty-ones at Cleveland. The deputy chaplain, John Jarvis, asked me to help him and we've organised talks, events and Alpha courses. I was also invited into Northallerton Youth Offenders Institute, North Yorkshire, by the Salvation Army, who have a presence in the prison. The governor, Norman Griffin, is keen to have me there. He's a brilliant governor, very fair, and makes sure he knows all the facts of a situation, without taking sides.

I'd been trying without success to get into Wealstun, West Yorkshire, to visit John Farrow, a prisoner there. One day I was telling my story in Hassockfield, when someone called Martin Narey approached me. 'Gram, if there's ever anything I can do to help, let me know,' he said.

'Do you ever go into Wealstun?' I asked him. He told me he went in now and again. The following week, I got an invitation to go. I'd been trying to get in for three years! I then found out that Martin was chief executive of the National Offender Management Service (England and Wales) and he'd put a good word in for me; he's chief executive of Barnardos now. I was really grateful for his help.

I come across a lot of lads in prison I've known from my old life. One of those was Tommy Harrison, who I used to sell counterfeit gear for. Tommy was a well-respected figure in the criminal world. One Crown Court judge described him as 'Teeside's elder statesman of the underworld'. Tommy was in Holme House and came to the chapel when I was giving my talk. The way Jesus had changed me really spoke to him and we spent a lot of time chatting, praying and reading the Bible. By the time I saw him again, I could tell he'd had a real encounter with God. He was a different person.

However, my work has not been without its problems. I was told that I was under investigation for bringing drugs into Wealston. I asked Terry McCarthy, the head chaplain at Holme House, and some of the police I knew what I should do. They advised me to see the governor of security. He called me, asking what I wanted to see him about. I told him what had been said and he reassured me that it wasn't true.

When I first started going into the prisons, some of the officers wondered why I was going in the staff entrance rather than in with the prisoners. A lot of them still can't get their head round it; they think a leopard doesn't change its spots. Some still don't think I'm genuine, but I know I have to be patient and let the difference in my life speak to them. It's hard at times. I've sometimes been criticised and told my teaching is rubbish and I'm not an ordained minister; what right did I have preaching about Jesus? Christians often get opposition when doing something for God, but God has removed a lot of those people that have got in the way of His work. I just need to focus on what He's given me to do.

I've also been involved with Alpha for Prisons and Caring for Ex-Offenders, two ministries run by Holy Trinity Church, Brompton. Paul Cowley and Emmy Wilson, who head up these ministries, are brilliant. Paul's now a great friend of mine. Emmy is absolutely awesome – she calls me 'big brother' and I call her 'little sister'.

I joined them on a great three-day mission in Maghaberry Prison, Belfast. There were twenty-two lads there that were already full of Jesus, which really blessed us. I've also been in Shepton Mallet, Somerset and Wandsworth, London.

When we first arrived at Shepton Mallet, I was gutted. They wouldn't let me in.

'What are you going to do?' Emmy asked me.

'The Lord must want me here for something,' I told her.

I decided to get the bus to nearby Glastonbury and, as I waited in the queue, God prompted me to talk to a couple of lads nearby. As I spoke to them, I found out they were going in the same direction, so I suggested sharing a taxi. On the journey, I told them my story and found out they'd just got out of a Young Offenders Institute. I thought maybe that was why God had wanted me there instead of in the prison. But I wasn't ready to give up yet.

*   *   *   *   *

'Let me in, let me in!' I was banging my fists on the walls of Shepton Mallet jail. People nearby were staring at me. I didn't care.

When I'd got back to the prison, I had another hour to wait for the team. God prompted me to walk round the jail – like the Israelites had walked around the walls of Jericho – and bang on the walls. Surely, something would happen now?

But it didn't. They still refused me entry the next morning. I was gutted; I really wanted to talk to the lads. I sat on the bank outside, wondering what to do, when a guy walked past in a Burberry mac and suit. I felt prompted to speak to him.

'Hi there, mate. How are you doing?' I said.

'Hi, have you just got out? Are you waiting for a lift?'

I told him I'd come from Middlesbrough to help Holy Trinity Brompton run a mission, but I'd been refused entry because of my criminal record. 'Don't go anywhere,' he said. 'In fact, follow me and wait outside.'

I waited and suddenly the big doors that let in the prison vans opened. Behind one of the vans were Emmy and the prison chaplain. Emmy had a massive smile on her face.

'You can come in, brother!' she shouted.

It turned out that the guy I'd been talking to was the governor. He told the gate off for refusing me entry when I'd travelled all this way to share my story. I walked through the gate with a big grin on my face. Emmy has told that story round the world; I'd spent so many years wanting to get out of jail and now I was spending all my time wanting to get back in – in fact, I even bang on the walls to be let in!

I help out with the three-day missions every year. I've been interviewed on stage at Holy Trinity Brompton three times and spoke at the largest ever Alpha supper party on Clapham Common, with nearly 3,000 people there. That's the amazing thing about God: He takes you from the guttermost to the uttermost. Not long before, I was an alcoholic tramp waiting to die and now I was preaching the gospel to people from Knightsbridge. Sometimes it just doesn't seem real; I can't believe the way God's changed my life.

I've seen hundreds of people make a commitment to Jesus over the years. They often find in prison that when they are in the chapel and in God's presence, they feel very peaceful and safe, even the really hard lads. I tell them they don't have to watch their backs while they are there. But a lot of them turn away from God, especially when they come under peer pressure or are bullied on the wings. However, I've also seen lads get out with totally different lives. I still hear about what happens to them, especially because I know so many people in Middlesbrough.

So what's the difference between the successes and the ones who fall away? It's the ones who make time with Jesus a daily habit, as I have taught them. One of the most powerful things they can do to grow as Christians is to read the Bible every day. I always encourage them to start small, by reading one verse a day, writing it out on a piece of paper, carrying it round and re-reading it. That way it becomes part of their mind and heart. It's those small steps of growth that matter. I wouldn't expect them to read and memorise hundreds of pages, especially words and ideas they don't understand, in the same way you wouldn't expect to learn bricklaying by laying 1,000 bricks a day. You start with a few bricks at a time.

You know which ones have taken that advice; they look different, they act differently and their relationship with God remains strong when they leave prison. That's because the Bible is God's way of speaking to us and a guide for how we should live our lives. But more than that, it actually changes us. If I read a book about David Beckham, it wouldn't change my heart or my direction. It might give me false hope: I'll never be like David Beckham. But I can read this book about Jesus and become like Him, because it's the living Word, not just dead words on a page. That's why statistics show that the Bible has remained the world's bestseller for so many years. No other book is as precious and as powerful.

The wonderful thing about God is that He's not just

interested in what you can do for Him, but in your whole life. He has provided for all my family's needs, especially our home. When we got married, we lived in my flat at first, but we were soon expecting our first child and needed more space. I wanted to stay in Whinney Banks, but we couldn't find a house in that area to rent. Natasha's hairdresser mentioned that she was renting out a house in the Salters Lane estate, Stockton, but the tenants still had twelve months on their lease. However, a couple of months later, she phoned to say it was actually six months, not twelve – and they had decided to leave.

I wanted to stay in Middlesbrough, but Stockton is actually much better for us. It's closer to the motorway and I don't have to travel through Middlesbrough to get to it and our church is just round the corner. It's central to everywhere I need to travel to.

But it didn't end there. One morning, I was up at 6am praying, when I felt God telling me to find a mortgage and get on the property ladder. That's not possible, I thought. I must be blacklisted by every finance company in the area. I'd ripped them all off.

I had started working for the church by then on a very small salary and I was really living by faith, but every day, for the next month, God told me the same thing.

'Natasha, I think the Lord wants us to buy this house,' I said eventually.

She wasn't sure. The house needed a lot of money spending on it. However, we found one nearby, on Winpole Road, for £59,000. We felt it was the right one for us and visited our financial advisor, Geoff Bollins. I'd first met Geoff when I was telling my story at his church. For some reason, I felt compelled to talk about when I'd broken into my secondary school and nearly got caught by the caretaker, Mr Bollins.

Afterward, Geoff came up with his wife, Chris, and told me that Mr Bollins was his dad! He'd become a Christian just before he died and he would have been delighted to see what had happened to me.

Geoff managed to secure us a mortgage, much to my astonishment, and we moved in. A few years later, the Lord started talking to me again about moving to a bigger house; at that time Natasha had to go upstairs every time I had meetings, which was unfair on her. We also wanted an extra bedroom so that both our families could come and stay. Our house was sold for £135,000. However, houses on the estate where we really wanted to live were at least £240,000. We didn't have the money.

'You're looking on the wrong estate. There's a house somewhere else I want to give you.'

I knew God was speaking to me, but I was disobedient and carried on looking in the same area. However, one day, driving through another estate, we spotted a 'For sale' sign in a back garden that could be seen from the main road. 'Tasha, look at that. That's our house!'

'How do you know?' she said.

'I just know.'

We went to speak to the owners, Pam and Harry. As soon as Pam opened the door, I said: 'You're going to think I'm a nutter, but I'm a born-again Christian and we believe God's going to give us this house.'

'Good,' she said. 'It's been up for sale for sixteen months.'

I asked why the sign had only just gone up and she said the wind had blown it down the previous year. Without knowing the price, I told her I could only pay £195,000. She said it wasn't enough – her husband wouldn't go lower than £200,000. It had already been dropped from £230,000. I knew God would give it to us, but they rejected our offer. We were on holiday in

Scarborough when we received a call to say that the house had been sold. The buyers had offered the full asking price and had sold their own house. Natasha was crying.

I went to visit Pam and Harry.

'I'm sorry to say this, but don't get your hopes up,' I told them. 'This is our house and you won't sell it to anyone else.'

The deal fell through.

We got another phone call saying it had been sold again for the asking price. I was back on their doorstep. Harry was getting sick of me by now – in fact he'd informed his solicitor that I was harassing him.

The deal fell through and they finally accepted our offer. We moved into our new house, in Fairfield, on 8 November 2005 – bought for £35,000 less than the original asking price.

Looking back, we can see God's hand in all of this. If we hadn't got onto the property ladder when He told us to, we would never have had the deposit for this house. But the real blessing was that both our families could come and stay with us whenever they wanted. It also allowed my mam a closer look at my new life. It really made a difference.

The week it all changed for my mam was quite a difficult one. She was staying with us and there had been quite a bit of conflict, with arguments and badly behaved children. But as we drove her to the airport, she put her hand on my knee and said, 'Do you know what, son? How do I get Jesus into my heart?' She had tears in her eyes.

'Mam, do you really want Him in your heart?'

'Yes I do.'

So Natasha, Caleb and I all put our hands on her – I remembered to keep my eyes open because I was driving – and prayed. There in the car, travelling down the A1, my mam asked Jesus into her life. God really touched her and she was crying. Since then I've seen a real change in her; she's so much more relaxed and content. But it was only when we obeyed God and had the faith to move into a bigger house that she was able to see my relationship with Jesus on a daily basis. For that alone, the house is worth every penny.

She also needed time to forgive me for everything I'd done in the past and, in the end, it's only Jesus who can supernaturally heal the pain. I often say to the lads in the prison that when I had my finger chopped off, it really hurt the next day, but sometimes even now when I cut my nails, I forget that there isn't a nail there. That's because there's no pain behind it any more. Forgiveness is a bit like that, but it's only when God heals the pain that it makes a difference. It's taken me a long time to forgive some people – especially those that attacked me when I was a tramp – and I was a Christian for a number of years before I could forgive my dad. God didn't heal my body all at once; it was two years after I became a Christian before He healed my eyes – and He doesn't always heal our emotions all at once. It's a growing and a learning process and a process of elimination.

About five years ago, I was doing a car boot sale for my mam when I found something that had puzzled me for twenty years. At the bottom of an old tea chest lay my nana's purse. I remembered how upset and angry I'd been when she died and it disappeared; both my family and the police blamed me. I'd desperately tried to find out who had taken it to prove I hadn't done it; I even went to the hospital to find the ambulance drivers who had taken her body away. Had it been them?

But now, here it was. All the memories came back, but not the emotions. I'd forgiven those who had blamed me and God had healed me of the pain. I was free.

My wider family recognise that my life is different and they've seen God at work. Once I felt God telling me to ring my uncle and he told me that the doctor had just found a lump on his bowel. He was really worried about it. I prayed for him on the phone and asked him to put his hand on his stomach where the lump was. He did so and I told him that the lump had gone. When he went to hospital the next day, it had completely disappeared. He'd seen the power of God at work.

But God doesn't just stop at healing family relationships – those you are expected to love; he wants to heal the rift between you and your enemies – those you are expected to hate. When I was fighting at football matches, one of the enemy gangs was the Inter City Firm (ICF), the West Ham crew who had slashed my face. I met one of them in Shepton Mallet – a big, black guy called Steve.

'What are you doing here?' he grunted at me.

I told him and he walked off without another word.

I shared my story with the lads and he came to sit with me at break. He said it was brilliant. He told me he had been in the ICF; he'd shot someone and had been inside for eighteen years. When I asked the lads to stand up if they wanted to make a commitment to Jesus, he was on his feet. It was fantastic; from us both battling each other in different gangs, and his initial hostility when I first came, to a transformed life as a new Christian. He even gave me a hug when I went. We wouldn't have done that twenty years ago!

Another rift that God has gradually healed is that with the police. I was hardly their favourite person. Years of crime and battling with them to resist arrest had left them all very suspicious of me, even after I became a Christian. At first they used to bust my door down. I thought they were trying to wind me up. They even arrested me once for selling heroin. A member of the Ward family, Gerard, was about thirteen at the time and had to be interviewed at the station, and the police asked me to come with him. He needed to be accompanied by an adult, but they wanted to speak to me as well. When I got there, I was locked in a cell and later interviewed. I knew I hadn't done anything wrong and the accusation, which then changed to handling stolen goods, was dropped. However, sitting praying in that cell I felt no anger at all – just peace. Even though I was locked up, I knew I was free, and nobody could take that away. But they couldn't get their heads round my attitude. Once, when I was walking down the street, a police van pulled up.

'What are you up to, Gram? Where are you going?' said the officer in the driving seat.

'I'm a Christian now. I'm going to start helping people.'

'We'll believe that when we see it. And when you fall, we'll get you.'

I walked nearer to the van. He looked worried, and wound the window up.

'Do you know what I'm going to do for you tonight?' I said, leaning towards the van. 'I'm going to pray for you.'

'You what?' he shouted. 'You're going to pray for us?' Suddenly they shot off in the van and I realised then that I had something very different now. It was humility and love.

Over the years they've started to realise that what I have is genuine. I was invited to the mayor's chambers once, to Stop and Search, a debate with CID and the police. I had the chance to share a bit of my past. But the biggest shock was the fact that I ended up baptising one of them.

*   *   *   *   *

Brian McCarthy had been doing his usual shift when he was called to the Longlands area of Middlesbrough. Apparently there was a big guy in a yellow jumper kicking up a fuss in a chip shop. Guess who? When Brian came in, I apparently took his baton off him, then gave it back. I was a tramp at the time and I would often deliberately cause a riot so I could get locked up in a warm police cell for the night with some food. Sometimes I would even go to the station and jump up and down on a police car. Brian had to deal with me a few times over the years and was often in the interview room when I was being charged. However, I didn't meet him again until 1997. I was waiting in Middlesbrough bus station while Patrick Hinton went to the toilet, when Brian walked up.

'What are you doing here, Gram?' he asked.

I told him I was waiting for a friend and he took his hat and gloves off, a sign that he was being friendly. We chatted for a while and Patrick came back. He said, 'Do you know Gram, then? He's a poacher turned gamekeeper now, you know.' Patrick always introduced me like that.

Years later, Keith Howard, a member at our church said that there was a policeman attending who knew me. It was Brian. He'd become a Christian through Keith, who had been the karate instructor for the police force. Brian asked if I would baptise him with Keith. It was fantastic – there's something very powerful about an ex-con baptising a policeman. It's really spoken to the lads in the prison when they've seen it on video – although some of them can't quite believe it.

'How long did you hold him under for?' one of them once asked me.

But in the midst of all the joy of seeing lives changed, rifts healed and relationships restored, there is pain – the pain of what might have been and, in some cases, what never will be. Some have been lost for ever and others were on the dangerous downward spiral that I was once on, and would probably be dead before long. Despite all my efforts, it wasn't enough. I knew I had to do more. It was a huge risk, but it needed to happen. There was no other way.

My life was about to change again.

CHAPTER ELEVEN

SEEDS OF HOPE

'It's quite miraculous what God has done. Gram's not on the receiving end any more; he's giving out now and has had a remarkable impact on young men in the prisons. It's extraordinary what he's done.'
Mike Horner, Tees Valley Community Church

I sat staring at the coffin, tears pouring down my face. Everyone else had left and I was alone, watching a digger drop earth into the open grave.

'That's it. He's gone.'

He was just twenty-four years old.

I'd known Michael since he was about seven. He was a likeable but mischievous lad. I'd tried my best to help, but the pull of his drug habit was too strong. They found him dead in a garden shed two weeks after leaving prison; he'd been there for three days. He'd left a family, a girlfriend and a baby.

I was devastated. 'Lord, I really, really need Your help right now. I don't know how to deal with this,' I cried out, as I sat by his graveside.

Seeing lives destroyed – especially those that have known the love of God and rejected it – is the most agonising part of my job. I've seen so many make really good progress growing in their relationship with God, sometimes for many years, but then they get out of prison and slowly but surely, they start slipping away. Prison cocoons you from the outside world, keeping you away from a lot of temptation, but as soon as you get out, you want to do everything at once – including everything that will destroy you.

Lads are pressured from all sides. I try to teach them the value of saving sex for marriage and the blessing it brings, but a lot think that by living like this they are being wimpish, rather than strong Christians. They give in easily. Others are lured back into the excitement of crime or the quick release of drink and drugs. Sin is such a deceiver. The devil's tactics are to make things look good, when really they are bad. The Bible says he comes as an angel of light. Behind it is all darkness ... Satan is like a wolf in sheep's clothing.

The more I read the Bible, the more I became convinced that Satan, the devil, was real. It made sense that if there was a source of good – God – then there had to be a source of evil – the devil. But people are more ready to blame God when things go wrong, rather than the devil. Looking at my former life, I can now see a supernatural force of evil at work. Many times, without realising it, I invited it into my life by dabbling in the occult and by taking part in that strange 'spiritualist' ceremony that caused me to see evil figures and hear voices. I'm convinced that for thirty-two years I was under the influence of the devil without knowing it. He did everything he could to try and destroy me.

But it's the deaths that are the hardest to deal with. I've been to forty-four funerals so far and many of them were friends. A lot died without ever having a chance to know Jesus. My mate Wogo killed himself in 1994. He was doing life for murder when he escaped from Franklin Prison. He read up on appendicitis and faked the symptoms; as there were no hospital wings in those days, he was taken to the University Hospital of North Durham. He'd broken his own thumbs in preparation, and when the prison guard went to the toilet, Wogo slipped his handcuffs and climbed out of the window. My house was under surveillance, but he was caught in London. He was given an extra ten years on top of his life sentence. Not long after, they found him hanging in his cell. His brother, Patrick, also killed himself. If only they could have had what I have, it would have been so different.

All the deaths have been tragic. One lad, Stuart, became almost like a son to me. He was fifteen years old, homeless and living on a roof. Pete Conroy got to know him and he eventually became a Christian. He spent a lot of time at my house. We became close and he really respected me. But he moved away and started slipping back into his old life. I got a call telling me he'd been found dead from a suspected overdose.

It's at times like these that I really need to throw myself on the Lord. He comforts me and removes the sadness and pain. I know I've got a direct line to God and I can tap into that power at any time, but sometimes I have so many unanswered questions: 'Why did it go wrong? Why has that lad gone back to drugs? Why did this one die?' But in the end, I get on my knees and cry out to God. Sometimes I'll get up at 5am and lay in front of the fire, praying and weeping over what's happened. Often I'll lay awake at night when my body is exhausted and wants to sleep, but my mind is churning. But I always know that God's with me and try to keep my eyes on Him and not the problem. I'll never have all the answers, but God gives me the strength to keep going.

When the prison work started to build up, I felt prompted by God to set up a proper ministry. I had no idea how to go about it. As I prayed, God gave me the words and I wrote on three A4 pieces of paper and took them to the leaders in my church. They invited me to their elders' meeting and I got a call that night to say that they were amazed at what I'd written. They knew it was from God and they believed it was important for the church to support it. I raised £850 a month straightaway from supporters and the church made up the shortfall. In October 2000, Emmanuel Prison Ministries was born.

Now six years later it was about to change again. That day, watching Michael's coffin disappear under the soil I was so moved, but felt so helpless. There must be something more I could do. I'd always felt like a one-man band up to this point, doing everything alone. I regularly travelled more than 700 miles a week, often doing twelve-hour days, but it was never enough. There had to be another way – a better way.

One day, our senior church leader was talking to me about doing more youth work and fewer days in the prison, when suddenly, something moved across my eyes. It was the words: 'For such a time as this.' I even heard it being said. What on earth was that about? I didn't recognise the phrase from anywhere.

I couldn't find it in my Bible so I went to see church member Bob Kier, who's almost like a walking Bible with the amount of knowledge he has. He knew immediately that it was from the book of Esther, chapter 4 verse 14. It's not a book I would normally think of reading but as I read it and prayed for two hours that night, a new ministry was birthed.

After that, it was a process of confirmation. God will usually confirm a big move in several ways. While on holiday at Legoland, Windsor, we needed some milk for Boaz one evening. The shop we went to was shut. So was the garage round the corner. I returned to the hotel, asking God why he'd sent me to two closed shops. In the middle of the road was where a big arrow had been – it had been blacked over with Tarmac, but you could still see the outline. Next to it was a big white arrow pointing the other way. The Lord said, 'Gram, I want to change the direction of what you are doing.' The next day, the Lord showed me a box of Lego and said: 'Gram, it's time to get the Lego out of the box. You've been in a box and unless you get out, you can't make anything.'

I knew exactly what he meant. I'd been part of the church ministry, which provided my salary, but I'd been struggling on my own. Now God wanted me to start a new independent ministry that would involve more people and other churches. But it was scary. I was in a comfort zone, getting all my bills paid for. Where would the money come from?

I fasted and prayed about it for eight months and finally approached the church leadership in November 2006. I received the last of my salary in February 2007, but the church generously paid me until April when the charity Sowing Seeds Ministries was officially launched.

God had given me the name about seven years earlier. I was in the chapel at Holme House one day, grumbling to myself and to God.

'No one sees anything I'm doing and no one appreciates me,' I moaned. 'That's it. I'm not coming here any more.'

'Who do you think you are?' God said to me. 'All you are is My light.' He told me to read Matthew 13, which was all about sowing seeds. God told me that's what I was called to do – sow seeds of hope and truth that others can water and help them to grow and flourish. I didn't really want to use that phrase for the charity; people might think it's all about me, being a Seed by name. But God showed me that it was what He wanted.

In November 2006, Albert Dicken, chairman of the Goshen Trust charity in our church, approached me. He didn't know anything about me leaving the church staff or starting the charity, but he offered to pay for a DVD to be made of my life, to support the work I was doing. But it meant that I had to return to a place where I had experienced my greatest ever sense of failure some fifteen years previously.

The company, Boro TV Ltd, wanted to film part of my story in Wakefield, but as soon as we arrived, it all came flooding back as clear as if it was yesterday. This was the one place I'd tried harder than any other time in my life to change. It was where I'd hit an off-duty policeman in a nightclub and got sent down for it. In my eyes, it represented my biggest ever failure.

As the camera crew set up the equipment, I sat on a bench, praying, remembering all the old feelings of loneliness and despair. Then God spoke to me: 'Everything without Me is a failure. You would have always failed without Me, but now you are in My arms, I'm going to help you be a success.' He then reminded me of a piece of Scripture in the Old Testament, Jeremiah chapter 29:

> 'For I know the plans I have for you,' declares the LORD, 'plans to prosper you and not to harm you, plans to give you hope and a future. Then you will call upon me and come and pray to me, and I will listen to you. You will seek me and find me when you seek me with all your heart.' (verses 11–13)

It was such a comfort for me. Years ago, I would have buried these feelings behind a mask, but God wants us to face issues head on and let Him deal with them. Sitting on that bench in Wakefield, God finally healed me of those feelings of failure.

My vision for Sowing Seeds Ministries is to have a team of people to befriend and support prisoners, both inside and when they are released. Often, prisoners come from the sheltered world of jail, with nothing but a discharge grant and their belongings in a clear bag with HMP stamped on it. They have to make their own way home. Lots of things can happen on the way home – if they have a home to go to. There might be someone outside in a big car with a nice fat wallet, ready to lure them back into a life of crime. My aim is for them to walk into a safe, structured environment that will encourage them to sort out their lives, find a home, work, friends and, more importantly, the hope and peace that only Jesus can give them.

It's a big vision. It's hard work, but I've got some strong support. It's exciting, but at times I've been fearful for my family. At this moment, I've got 48 per cent of my old wage and I don't know where the rest of the money will come from. If God doesn't pay the bills, they won't get paid. What will happen to my family? Will they end up homeless? But I have to remember that God loves my family much more than I ever could and I have to trust that He will look after them.

*   *   *   *   *

God continues to teach me how to be a good father and it's a daily learning process. I regularly remind my sons that I will always be there for them. I try to have regular father and son times with both of them and we benefit from that.

Caleb started asking about God when he was about four and he made a commitment to Jesus. He'll grow in his relationship with Jesus when he's older, but at the moment, if it's a choice between Spiderman and praying, Spiderman will win ... He's always had a temper problem and he's lashed out at a lot of people. He's as strong as a bull and would send other kids flying if he hit them. But he has also struggled to do things like write or fasten his shoelaces and used to get very frustrated. We knew something was wrong. Then Natasha read a book about dyspraxia, a condition that affects motor skills and balance. It feels a bit like trying to do something with your hands while wearing oven gloves. It sounded exactly like Caleb. The diagnosis in 2007 confirmed our suspicions.

Looking back, I now suspect I had the same condition as a child. I remember struggling in the same way, feeling frustrated and lashing out. Maybe that's part of the reason why I always wanted to be someone else – although there were a lot of other things going on as well. God's done a lot in me since then and I know God will heal our son.

I have a very heavy workload and I have to ensure that I make time for my family as well, but Natasha's absolutely brilliant in supporting the ministry and looking after the boys. She's been into prisons with me sometimes, supported some of the lads when they got out by welcoming them into our home, feeding them and washing their clothes, and has helped me with admin. I'm absolutely convinced that a lot of our blessings, both in the ministry and as a family, are because of Natasha's sacrifice.

When I met her, she'd just sold a café she owned. She'd had her own business, own flat, own car, her independence and had only been a Christian for about seven months. Then the Lord suddenly told her to marry me. She had to move away from her best friends, her sister and her mum, and live in a completely new area. She gave up a lot to support me; she's been there for me 100 per cent and stood by me through all the change and upheaval. It's not just about what I've done, because I couldn't have done it without her strong support behind the scenes.

I'm really hopeful for the future because God is in it. But looking back, I can see His fingerprints on my life even before

I knew Him: the time I was beaten in revenge when I mugged a taxi driver – I was left for dead and accidentally discovered by a dog walker at 5am; the time I believe God stopped the policeman getting killed by Wogo; the spell in prison during my bench years that I believe stopped me getting cirrhosis of the liver; my suicide attempt when the police found me – they never patrol at 3am, but this time they did. And God prompted those Christians to talk to me on my bench when I was a hopeless alcoholic. They were then around to pray for me when I'd slipped into a coma.

There are times when I hate my old life, but I also believe that it's now the greatest tool Jesus has given me to reach out to others. It's the proof that God can transform somebody and it can't be proven wrong. There are plenty of people that can testify to the genuine change in me. There are hundreds in Holme House alone that know me – more in Middlesbrough. I've told my story so many times, but if it was all a lie, there are plenty of people that would quickly pull me up on it. It's hard to keep a blag up; if I was preaching the gospel one minute, then going out clubbing, getting drunk and fighting the next, it would soon be all round the town.

I know God can change lives, if I continue to be obedient, but I don't always get it right. One time, I hesitated in telling a man in a petrol station that Jesus loved him. I'd been doing a mission in Oxford and we stopped to get some sweets and drinks. As I walked to the counter, the lad looked surprised, especially as I had 'Jesus' written across my head in face paint. I felt God say to me, 'Tell him I love him.' I thought I was imagining it, so I ignored it. As I left, God said, 'How much do you love Me? You won't even tell him for Me.' I put my stuff in the car and thought that maybe I would just give the guy a tract. My friends had got the car running and I said to them, 'I just need to go and tell this guy that Jesus loves him.' They turned the engine off!

I went back in. I found out later that the first time I went in, the guy thought he was going to get robbed. The second time I went in, with no carrier bag, he was fumbling around for the panic button. He was *definitely* going to get robbed now.

I said, 'Hi, mate. I've got something to tell you. I'm an ex-nutcase from Middlesbrough. I'm speaking at a church tomorrow. I want to tell you that Jesus loves you. I've come 200 miles to tell you that.'

He started crying. He came out in front of the counter and said, 'Tell me again.'

'Jesus loves you.'

He then told me his story: 'Five years ago, I went to university, but started going clubbing and using hard drugs. I got kicked out of uni, but pretended I was still there so my parents would send me money. I've owned up to them and I've been home eleven weeks now. My dad got me this job. I got up this morning feeling really low. My mum rang me as usual. Both my parents are Christians and Mum says the same thing every day – "Adam, Jesus loves you." This time I hung up and threw the phone so hard on the floor, it smashed. I opened the window and shouted out: "If You really ——— love me, You'd tell me." I believe He's done just that.'

I said to him, 'Do you want to know Jesus?'

In front of the queues of people waiting to pay for petrol, Adam prayed and gave his life to the Lord. He joined us on the mission picnic the next day.

God always leads us to the right place at the right time to do His work and, as long as we're obedient to Him, He'll use us. What if I'd have ignored what He told me to do that day? What would have happened to Adam?

Reading through my story, I pray that you believe and

have been touched by the evidence of what God has done in my life and continues to do in the lives of thousands. I wanted this book to bring hope; despite working long hours every week, I can't speak to everyone, or go into every prison, but this is a way for my story to reach people I might never have the chance to meet. It's not that I'm anything special, but what God has done in me is.

A close friend of mine, Bola, said he's read loads of stories about Christians. He likes the first half of the book, but not the bit when they find God. He doesn't believe it and thinks lads in prison become Christians to get parole. But he told me if he ever read my book, he'd believe it, because he knows there's something different about me. He's seen it.

That's the reality of God. My pastor, Phil Hillsdon, once introduced me and said, 'This sounds like a fairytale, but it's a real story.' It is real and around every corner, there are people like me who've made it because of Jesus. I'm not trying to force anyone to believe – neither is God. People have to make a personal decision for themselves, but I want everyone to know that the same God that has worked in me wants to work in you too. I spent so many years looking for the living among the dead, trying to find a reason for living in things that were shallow, meaningless and hopeless, and only truly found life when I became a Christian. God's taken me from being a chronic alcoholic criminal with no hope, just waiting to die, to someone who is completely alcohol and drug free, with a beautiful wife, wonderful children, lovely home, restored relationships with family and friends, and a powerful purpose in my life to set the captives free.

How could I possibly keep quiet about that?

CHAPTER TWELVE

CAPTIVES RELEASED

NOW HEAR FROM THREE 'RELEASED CAPTIVES' ...

TOMMY HARRISON

I threw my Bible onto the floor of my cell. What was the point of it all?

I was in prison again. I'd just lost my appeal and felt completely abandoned and hopeless – abandoned even by God.

Going to church was part of my childhood. My grandmother was very religious. I was a believer, but I never really had an encounter with God. Somewhere along the way, I lost what little faith I had.

I started getting involved in crime at an early age, stealing and receiving stolen goods and later got involved in selling top fashion copy clothing. That's when Gram started working for me.

I'd known Gram since he was a boy. He was a good friend of my son, Lee. He was a regular on the scene, always dressed smartly in top designer gear, surrounded by crowds of people, including women; the Michael Caine of Middlesbrough!

The copy clothing was big business and Gram made quite a lot of money from it. However, one day he took a large amount of clothing and never came back. I was disappointed, rather than annoyed. I had a lot of trust in Gram. However, a month later, he turned up, full of remorse and apologies. I respected him for that. I didn't have to go looking for him. He agreed to work off what he owed me.

I got a two-and-a-half-year stretch and when I came out the scene was buzzing – so was the clothes business. Drugs were becoming more common and I often saw Gram around town, drunk and off his head. He would turn up at pubs selling gear to buy drink and drugs. Some people would wait until he was desperate and buy his stuff for next to nothing. I sometimes bought it off him to stop him getting ripped off.

Later, when he was living rough on the bench, I often tried to talk to him, but it was a waste of time. He was gone. The last I heard of him was that he'd been taken to hospital and might not come out.

*　　*　　*　　*　　*

'Dad, there's Gram!' We'd just pulled into a service station when we spotted him. He was smiling and talking to people coming out of the café. He had a Bible in his hand.

'Gram, what's the scam now? What move have you got on?' I asked him.

'None! I'm a changed man. The Lord saved me and I want to help others.'

I laughed at him. 'Come on, let's buy you something to eat and have the crack.'

'No, I'm busy here,' he said. He even refused money when I offered it.

In later years, I was on remand in Holme House when my son came rushing over.

'Dad, Gram's in the chapel. He's telling everyone how the Lord saved him. He's a different man.'

I went to listen to the talk and I was amazed. The old Gram Seed and the new one were worlds apart. He convinced me that it was real and made me want to change my life and find my faith again.

I attended the Alpha course, and the chapel three times a week, and started praying and reading the Bible. I had one-to-one sessions with Gram, where he taught me about the Bible. He's shown me a new way of life and how to forgive. He's supported me through some really bad times and given me comfort and hope.

Now I pray and read the Bible every morning before I get out of bed. Reading about the apostle Paul and how he kept his faith has been a particular encouragement. It's helped me to push on and not let anyone or anything get in the way of my belief in God.

Even though I'm still in prison, Jesus has really helped me to cope. He's brought an inner peace and taught me to take every day as it comes. I've particularly been encouraged when God's answered my prayers. I've prayed for my sons – one is in Thailand and one is in prison – and when I've phoned home, I've found out that my prayers have been answered. I know now that Someone is always with me.

I'm hoping to help Gram in his ministry when I get out. I'm particularly keen to set up a youth club for meetings, particularly as young people don't hear about religion in schools. I want to put something back into society. Gram's proved to me that all the material things I valued in the past mean nothing; all you need is that inner peace and contentment that comes through faith in God. I could never repay Gram for what he's done for me.

'Tommy was a well-respected figure in the criminal world, with global criminal connections. He's also been written about in a number of books about crime in the north-east and was referred to by one judge as "Teesside's elder statesman of the underworld".'

Gram Seed

*   *   *   *   *

LIAM

'God, if You are there, help me!'

I was in a desperate situation. I was at King's Cross, London – no money, on the run from the police and was nearly out of methadone. I didn't know what to do.

I'd been a drug addict since I was a teenager and by the time I was twenty-three, I was hooked on heroin. I'd been in and out of prison since I was seventeen. I was always fighting and getting into trouble. I'd had quite a dysfunctional upbringing where fighting and drinking were the norm for my parents. I was affected by it and grew up believing violence was the way to solve problems. I took drugs because I wanted something to take me out of reality.

By the time I got to King's Cross, I'd been living on the streets of Oxford for several weeks, getting involved in crime. I had nothing and nowhere to go. As soon as I cried out to God, it came to me to go and give myself up. It made so much more sense.

At the station, I got talking to the desk sergeant who told me he was a Christian. I asked for a book to read and in the box of books was a Bible.

'Do you have faith?' the sergeant asked me.

'No.'

'Give me five minutes. I'll come and chat to you.'

I thought that was unusual. I was going through

withdrawal and when he came to see me, I told him how fed up I was. He told me God could help me and Christ was the answer. He offered to pray for me and when he laid hands on me, it felt like I'd been hit by a bolt of lightning. Something was different and I knew things were going to change.

I'd learned something about God during a previous sentence; I'd started going to a chapel group. My girlfriend, Helen, started going to a local Anglican church and ended up getting confirmed. I knew about the Holy Spirit and God was starting to break through, but I was still using heavily.

Six weeks into an eighteen-month sentence in Holme House Prison, I heard a talk by an ex-gangster in the chapel. He'd become a Christian and was now free from his past. He offered to pray for me and as soon as he laid hands on me, I had another powerful encounter with God. I really wanted to go for it then and turn away from my previous lifestyle. When I told everyone on the wing what happened, they thought I was off my head, but some of them wanted to experience the same thing.

Not long after, I met Gram in the chapel. We clicked straight away and we arranged to meet a number of times. He really helped me and supported me and, more importantly, he was there to meet me at the gate when I got out. I'd heard of so many people getting lost between the gate and the bus stop and getting sideswiped; everything you've gained then stays at the gate. So much comes against you. But for me, there was a safety net there. Gram took me to the Teen Challenge rehab and it took me a year and a half to get clean.

Now I'm married to Helen and we have a son and a daughter. We have our own home and I've got a good job.

I'm working with someone now who knew me before I became a Christian. He said I've become a different person. I know I couldn't have done it without God, and Gram played such a big part in that. It's such an important ministry that he's involved in.

I would say to anyone who is reading this book and thinking about God: just go for it, don't give it a second thought. You'll always have Someone there to rely on who won't let you down. His name is Jesus.

*   *   *   *   *

PAUL

I sat by my uncle's grave praying to anyone who would listen – dead mates, my dog, my uncle. Surely, someone was out there who could hear me?

I was trying to escape a bad situation where I was going to kill someone. I didn't want to end up back in prison, but it was bound to happen. I'd been inside so many times over the years, just like my dad.

My dad had been in prison all his life and my mum was a drug addict. Growing up, surrounded by drugs, it was inevitable that I'd follow in her footsteps. By the age of fifteen, I was a drug dealer. I thought I had it all together, but my life was a cycle of drugs and taking advantage of people. I was always depressed about my life and where I'd come from.

Within a year of that desperate graveside prayer, I was back in Bedford Prison. I met some Christians and one lady in particular, who was in her fifties, had something in her – the only way I could explain is, it was like she was doing back flips inside! I didn't understand it but I wanted what she had.

After that, every time I was in prison I met a Christian. In 2001 I went on a course called 'Why Jesus?' and said the sinner's prayer. It wasn't long after that when I met Gram.

Gram really helped me to have a deeper understanding of God and to me he was an example of who Jesus was. I had such a lot of questions … Gram always said there was no one who asked as many as me! I was constantly searching for answers. One of my issues was that the Christians I'd met didn't really have a clue about my life, but Gram had been there, seen it and done it. He understood where I was coming from and that really helped me.

Soon after I got out, I met my wife, got married, and within a year we had our first baby. Now I work with people coming out of prison and one of the recent highlights was being asked to give a character reference for a kid at court.

I know that without Jesus there's no way I could keep my family together. I wouldn't have anything if it wasn't for Him. My life's different and I know it's not me that's done it.

I remember saying to Gram one day that I was terrified that God wasn't real and my life had no meaning; I might as well go back to drugs. He told me to just dive in and go for God and I did. I woke up the next morning and all those questions were gone. They'd been answered.

At the end of the day, you don't get another go at life. I've tried crime and drugs and they haven't worked. Everyone sat in a prison cell knows that. I would encourage everyone to try Jesus – what have you got to lose? You only have to accept what's on offer. You won't regret it.

ADDITIONAL COMMENTS

Gram's not a one-off. God has millions of one-off incidents. What he does with each individual is unique and every story is different. Gram's one of thousands. Clearly he suffered as a result of his past; every individual suffers something as a result of sin done to him. Sin's contagious, but the truth is we're all individually responsible for getting over it, if we turn to the Lord and draw on his resources. Gram's simply grabbed the opportunity that God's given him.
Mike Horner, Tees Valley Community Church

It's a typical story of God's amazing grace. This same story is repeated many times in the lives of all sorts of people – drug addicts, alcoholics, prostitutes, prisoners, the suicidal. It's another powerful story that proves that no one's beyond the reach of God. He can work with any raw material.
Martin Ruddick, evangelist

A lot of people focus on the miracle of Gram coming out of a coma, but to me, the greater miracle by far is that he's never touched a drink, drugs or a cigarette since then. No one had a clue what to do about the drug problem on Teeside and there were no programmes or support networks for addicts. … I think God plucked him out of his situation and chose him to take that message to others.
Pete Conroy, evangelist

Being around Gram is like being around Jesus. I love going into prison with him. Each time, his testimony becomes more powerful and no one can doubt his life is a miracle. He has such compassion for the prisoners and speaks with such incredible authority and humour. I know there will be hundreds of people, not just prisoners, who will look back and thank God for meeting Gram. He's one of the 'Oaks of Righteousness, a planting of the Lord for the display of his splendour'.

Emmy Wilson, ministry pastor, Holy Trinity Brompton

I first met Gram about seven years ago whilst I was speaking at an Alpha Conference in the North East of England. After getting over the initial shock of his sheer size and power, he told me his story. I instantly became enthralled by all that Gram had been through, and by how the Lord had changed him.

In all my years of prison work I have never seen a man so captivated by the love of Jesus. The compassion and love that he shows to prisoners and ex-offenders, not to mention his determination to help them adapt to their new lives, is almost supernatural. He is truly a testimony to the scripture: 'If any man be found in Christ, he is a new creation, the old has gone and the new has come.' – 2 Corinthians 5:17. I count Gram as a real man of God.

Revd Paul Cowley, executive director,
Social Transformation, Alpha International

OTHER COMMENTS

(taken from Gram's website www.sowingseeds.org.uk)

Gram Seed is a valid asset to Hassockfield STC as he gives spiritual guidance to young people who are in the most traumatic times in their lives. Gram has helped young people understand their situation and continually gives them advice and guidance of how to manage their feelings and behaviours. The young people have a lot of respect for Gram and speak very highly of him as they feel that they can talk to him as they have issues of common ground. Gram does bring a special quality to his work with the young people and has benefited service delivery greatly within Hassockfield STC.

Jane Caird, on behalf of the Social Work team at Hassockfield
Secure Training Centre

Gram is a big man with a big heart for others who share the lifestyle he once lived. His is a story of eventual redemption after years of violence, substance abuse and decline. It is a narrative which might well have ended in death when Gram went into a coma ... instead we have a real-life miracle of a changed life. Now Gram wants nothing more than that others share that experience, that same miracle for themselves – the miracle of God working in their lives, challenging and transforming.'
Terry McCarthy, HMP Holme House

It has been my privilege to work on a number of occasions with Gram. He has been a much appreciated visitor to the chaplaincy groups and Alpha course ... his story always captivates his listeners and his experience of being where they are opens their minds to the credibility of the gospel message ... his words have always had an impact. Gram's genuine love for prisoners, for the Word of God and his desire to be obedient to the direction of the Holy Spirit shine through everything he does. I pray God's blessing on his continued ministry.
**Major Carol Young, Salvation Army,
Northallerton Outreach Centre**

SOWING SEEDS MINISTRIES

Sowing Seeds Ministries is a Christian charity that exists to bring the love of Christ to prisoners and ex-offenders.

The charity has three main goals:

1. To bring hope to those in trouble with the law and help them find faith.
2. By helping them, so reduce crime.
3. To provide help and support for the families of people in prison; they also suffer.

The charity aims to raise enough funds, through individual donations and grants, to employ additional staff to assist with the ministry, find accommodation to serve as a halfway house for ex-offenders, and eventually purchase a farm to assist rehabilitation and teach employable skills.

Gram Seed says:

'We can give offenders everywhere hope that they can change the way they live and the faith to make it happen. If we can help prevent just one offender from mugging an old lady or breaking into your house or mine, we all live better lives. Your contribution is a down payment on a better future for all of us – in society, in faith and in the glory of the Lord.'

For further information and to make a donation, please contact:
Sowing Seeds Ministries, PO Box 821, Stockton-on-Tees, TS19 1FD. United Kingdom
Telephone: 01642 575157; mob: 07983 382888
Email: info@sowingseeds.org.uk **Website:** www.sowingseeds.org.uk
UK Registered Charity Number: 1118261
UK Registered Company Number: 6010713

OTHER USEFUL CONTACTS

Alpha offers the opportunity to explore the meaning of life.
To find out more, contact the Alpha team at Holy Trinity Brompton on 020 7052 0378, **email** htbalpha@htb.org.uk
Website: www.htb.org.uk/alpha

Teen Challenge. It is the mission of Teen Challenge to provide youth, adults and children with an effective and comprehensive faith-based solution to drug and alcohol addiction as well as other life-controlling problems.
For more information, contact the head office at 01269 842718.
Website: www.teenchallenge.org.uk

NATIONAL DISTRIBUTORS

UK: (and countries not listed below)
CWR, Waverley Abbey House, Waverley Lane, Farnham, Surrey GU9 8EP.
Tel: (01252) 784700 Outside UK (44) 1252 784700 Email: mail@cwr.org.uk

AUSTRALIA: KI Entertainment, Unit 21 317-321 Woodpark Road, Smithfield,
New South Wales 2164. Tel: 1 800 850 777 Fax: 02 9604 3699
Email: sales@kientertainment.com.au

CANADA: David C Cook Distribution Canada, PO Box 98, 55 Woodslee Avenue, Paris,
Ontario N3L 3E5. Tel: 1800 263 2664 Email: sandi.swanson@davidccook.ca

GHANA: Challenge Enterprises of Ghana, PO Box 5723, Accra.
Tel: (021) 222437/223249 Fax: (021) 226227 Email: ceg@africaonline.com.gh

HONG KONG: Cross Communications Ltd, 1/F, 562A Nathan Road, Kowloon.
Tel: 2780 1188 Fax: 2770 6229 Email: cross@crosshk.com

INDIA: Crystal Communications, 10-3-18/4/1, East Marredpalli,
Secunderabad – 500026, Andhra Pradesh. Tel/Fax: (040) 27737145
Email: crystal_edwj@rediffmail.com

KENYA: Keswick Books and Gifts Ltd, PO Box 10242-00400, Nairobi.
Tel: (254) 20 312639/3870125 Email: keswick@swiftkenya.com

MALAYSIA: Canaanland, No. 25 Jalan PJU 1A/41B, NZX Commercial Centre, Ara Jaya,
47301 Petaling Jaya, Selangor. Tel: (03) 7885 0540/1/2 Fax: (03) 7885 0545
Email: info@canaanland.com.my

Salvation Book Centre (M) Sdn Bhd, 23 Jalan SS 2/64, 47300 Petaling Jaya, Selangor.
Tel: (03) 78766411/78766797 Fax: (03) 78757066/78756360
Email: info@salvationbookcentre.com

NEW ZEALAND: KI Entertainment, Unit 21 317-321 Woodpark Road, Smithfield,
New South Wales 2164, Australia. Tel: 0 800 850 777 Fax: +612 9604 3699
Email: sales@kientertainment.com.au

NIGERIA: FBFM, Helen Baugh House, 96 St Finbarr's College Road, Akoka, Lagos.
Tel: (01) 7747429/4700218/825775/827264 Email: fbfm_1@yahoo.com

PHILIPPINES: OMF Literature Inc, 776 Boni Avenue, Mandaluyong City.
Tel: (02) 531 2183 Fax: (02) 531 1960 Email: gloadlaon@omflit.com

SINGAPORE: Alby Commercial Enterprises Pte Ltd, 95 Kallang Avenue #04-00,
AIS Industrial Building, 339420. Tel: (65) 629 27238 Fax: (65) 629 27235
Email: marketing@alby.com.sg

SOUTH AFRICA: Struik Christian Books, 80 MacKenzie Street, PO Box 1144,
Cape Town 8000. Tel: (021) 462 4360 Fax: (021) 461 3612
Email: info@struikchristianmedia.co.za

SRI LANKA: Christombu Publications (Pvt) Ltd, Bartleet House, 65 Braybrooke Place,
Colombo 2. Tel: (9411) 2421073/2447665 Email: dhanad@bartleet.com

USA: David C Cook Distribution Canada, PO Box 98, 55 Woodslee Avenue, Paris,
Ontario N3L 3E5, Canada. Tel: 1800 263 2664 Email: sandi.swanson@davidccook.ca

CWR is a Registered Charity – Number 294387
CWR is a Limited Company registered in England – Registration Number 1990308

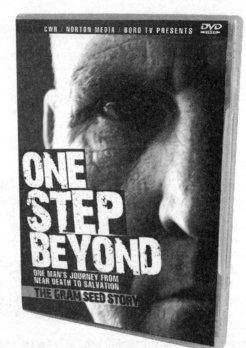

ONE STEP BEYOND DVD

This inspiring documentary of Gram's life includes re-enactments, and interviews with Gram, his family and some of those Jesus has touched through his ministry.
EAN: 5027957001084

Available from www.cwr.org.uk/store or local Christian bookshops

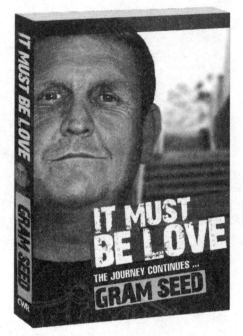

Courses and seminars

Publishing and new media

Conference facilities

Transforming lives

CWR's vision is to enable people to experience personal transformation through applying God's Word to their lives and relationships.

Our Bible-based training and resources help people around the world to:
• Grow in their walk with God
• Understand and apply Scripture to their lives
• Resource themselves and their church
• Develop pastoral care and counselling skills
• Train for leadership
• Strengthen relationships, marriage and family life and much more.

Our insightful writers provide daily Bible-reading notes and other resources for all ages, and our experienced course designers and presenters have gained an international reputation for excellence and effectiveness.

CWR's Training and Conference Centre in Surrey, England, provides excellent facilities in an idyllic setting – ideal for both learning and spiritual refreshment.

CWR Applying God's Word
to everyday life and relationships

CWR, Waverley Abbey House,
Waverley Lane, Farnham,
Surrey GU9 8EP, UK

Telephone: +44 (0)1252 784700
Email: info@cwr.org.uk
Website: www.cwr.org.uk

Registered Charity No 294387
Company Registration No 1990308